proclamation 2

Aids for Interpreting the
Lessons of the Church Year

easter

**George W. MacRae, S.J.
and
Charles P. Price**

series b

editors: Elizabeth Achtemeier · Gerhard Krodel · Charles P. Price

FORTRESS PRESS   PHILADELPHIA

Biblical quotations from the Revised Standard Version of the Bible, copyright 1946, 1952, © 1971, 1973 by the Division of Christian Education of the National Council of the Churches of Christ in the U.S.A., are used by permission.

Copyright © 1982 by Fortress Press

All rights reserved. No part of this publication may be reproduced, stored in a retrieval system, or transmitted in any form or by any means, electronic, mechanical, photocopying, recording, or otherwise, without the prior permission of the copyright owner.

Library of Congress Cataloging in Publication Data (Revised)

Main entry under title:

Proclamation 2.

 Consists of 24 volumes in 3 series designated A, B, and C which correspond to the cycles of the three year lectionary plus 4 volumes covering the lesser festivals. Each series contains 8 basic volumes with the following titles: Advent-Christmas, Epiphany, Lent, Holy Week, Easter, Pentecost 1, Pentecost 2, and Pentecost 3.
 CONTENTS: [etc.]—Series C: [1] Fuller, R. H. Advent-Christmas. [2] Pervo, R. I. and Carl III, W. J. Epiphany.—Thulin, R. L. et al. The lesser festivals. 4 v.
 1. Bible—Homiletical use. 2. Bible—Liturgical lessons, English.
[BS534.5.P76] 251 79-7377
ISBN 0-8006-4079-9 (ser. C, v. 1)

9390I81 Printed in the United States of America 1-4087

Contents

Editor's Foreword	5
The Resurrection of Our Lord, Easter Day	7
Easter Evening or Easter Monday	14
The Second Sunday of Easter	20
The Third Sunday of Easter	26
The Fourth Sunday of Easter	31
The Fifth Sunday of Easter	37
The Sixth Sunday of Easter	43
The Ascension of Our Lord	49
The Seventh Sunday of Easter	56

Editor's Foreword

Only in the last fifty years or so has the ancient character of the Christian celebration of Easter and Pentecost really been grasped, thanks to studies of such persons as F. E. Brightman, A. Baumstark, and G. Dix. Until the fourth century, Easter was a celebration of the cross, resurrection, exaltation, and coming of the Spirit as an undifferentiated whole, which went on for fifty days. "It is simply the feast of the Christian redemption, as the Jewish Passover was the feast of the Jewish redemption. . . . The Christian redemption was effected *by the cross and resurrection of Christ in combination,* viewed as a single act. There is no idea anywhere in christendom before the fourth century of a separate commemoration of the Passion on Good Friday and the Resurrection on Easter Sunday" (G. Dix, *The Treatise on the Apostolic Tradition of St. Hippolytus of Rome,* 1937; vol. 1, pp. 73–74). Pentecost, in turn, does not indicate the fiftieth day as such, but it denotes the entire period of fifty days, the "Great Fifty Days," during which the Christian Pascha was celebrated.

The present lectionary, on which this commentary is based, seeks to establish this newly recovered understanding of Easter by its concurrent emphasis on resurrection and the Spirit, its acceptance of the Johannine chronology for the coming of the Spirit on the first Easter evening, and its acknowledgment of the presence of the Spirit steadily thereafter through the series of readings from Acts, which is traditional Easter fare in place of an OT First Lesson. It is a time for participation in Christ through the sacraments (Luke 24, 1 John 5), for mutual indwelling of believers and their Lord in the Spirit (1 John), and for missionary outreach (Luke 24, Acts).

The liturgical Gospels in this season cover the events of the first Easter Day as recorded in Mark, Luke, and John. These lections are read on Easter 1, 2, and 3. Then we hear pertinent material from the Farewell Discourses in the Fourth Gospel on Easter 4, 5, 6, and 7. No mere chronology here! These are lections for a unitive celebration of Pascha, in the ancient sense, as both the exegesis and the homiletical interpretation insist.

The exegetical section of this volume was prepared by George W.

MacRae, S. J., Professor of NT at the Harvard Divinity School. He is the author of *Invitation to John,* the commentary on the Fourth Gospel in the Jerusalem Bible series, and *Faith in the Word,* the commentary on John in the Biblical Booklets series as well as editor of *The Word in the World,* essays in honor of Frederick L. Moriarty.

Because of a series of unforeseeable circumstances, the homiletical interpretation was written by the series editor himself, who is William Meade Professor of Systematic Theology at Virginia Seminary and author of *Principles in Christian Faith and Practice* and *Liturgy for Living.* He has sought to make theological formulation the mediating point between exegesis and sermon. Although he has had the preacher always in mind, the final work of shaping the sermon, always, remains with the preacher.

Alexandria, Va.   CHARLES P. PRICE

The Resurrection of Our Lord
Easter Day

Lutheran	Roman Catholic	Episcopal	Pres/UCC/Chr	Meth/COCU
Isa. 25:6–9	Acts 10:34, 37–43	Acts 10:34–43 or Isa. 25:6–9	Isa. 25:6–9	Isa. 25:6–9 or Acts 10:34–48
1 Cor. 15:19–28	Col. 3:1–4 or 1 Cor. 5:6–8	Col. 3:1–4 or Acts 10:34–43	1 Pet. 1:3–9	1 Cor. 15:19–28 or Col. 3:1–4
Mark 16:1–8 or John 20:1–9 (10–18)	John 20:1–9	Mark 16:1–8	Mark 16:1–8	John 20:1–18 or Mark 16:1–8

EXEGESIS

First Lesson: Isa. 25:6–9. The Book of Isaiah is a collection of prophetic oracles, hymns, narratives, and similar pieces compiled over a number of centuries in the name, and in some cases in the tradition, of the great preexilic prophet Isaiah. Our pericope is part of a late section of the work (chaps. 24—27), itself the result of compilation, which has traditionally been called the Apocalypse of Isaiah. It is not properly an apocalypse but emanates from the transition, which began soon after the Exile, from prophetic to apocalyptic eschatology. The early character of it is reflected in the fact that it is not entirely clear whether the coming cosmic destruction and victory (the events of "that day") are to take place in the future of history or beyond history, when by a new creative act God will renew the world.

The passage begins by describing, in traditional imagery, the eschatological banquet that is to take place on Mount Zion (see 24:23, of which our passage was originally a continuation interrupted by a psalm of thanksgiving). It should not be thought of as a messianic banquet in the strict sense, since in this passage, and throughout the Apocalypse of Isaiah, God does not act through an intermediary but as the Divine Warrior achieving the victory of his people directly and personally. The veil that he will remove, not only from Israel but from all nations, signifies the mourning of humanity for the sufferings that precede the Day of the Lord, chief among them death, which will then be conquered.

A notable feature of the passage is the balance between Jewish particularism—it is God's own people who will be vindicated—and prophetic universalism—all nations will attend the eschatological banquet, participate in the liberation from mourning and death, and acknowledge the sovereignty and saving power of God.

It is easy to understand the attractiveness of this passage for the celebration of Easter. The process began with St. Paul, who cites Isa. 25:8a in his discussion of resurrection (1 Cor. 15:54).

Second Lesson: 1 Cor. 15:19–28. The focus of Paul's long discussion in 1 Corinthians 15 is on the eschatological resurrection of the dead, not directly on the resurrection of Jesus. He is arguing in a context of some Corinthian Christians who deny that there is a (future) resurrection of the dead. His argument, as our pericope clearly shows, is centered on both the fact and the futurity of resurrection—for Christians. Paul says nothing of a general resurrection of all humanity. Yet the whole argument is an important discussion of the resurrection of Jesus, which is proclaimed in the Christian gospel, for it is the resurrection of Jesus that grounds the certainty of the resurrection of the dead. It is characteristic of Paul's understanding of the gospel message about Jesus that it speaks of human life and hope: Jesus "was put to death for our trespasses and raised for our justification" (Rom. 4:25).

V. 19 easily lends itself to misunderstanding: it is not even certain whether the word "only" applies to "hope" or (more likely) to "this life." In any case, as the whole of 1 Corinthians shows, the statement is not a denigration of this life, but it is a reminder that there is more.

Paul uses two arguments here to relate the resurrection of Christ to the resurrection of those who belong to Christ. The image of "first fruits" implies that the whole harvest is to follow. It is probably derived from the Israelite sacrificial system—the practice of consecrating the first fruits of the harvest to God—though no specific offering is referred to here. The second argument is an important one for Paul's understanding of Christ (see Rom. 5:12–20). It hinges on the role of Christ as a man representative of humanity in the sense that Adam was. If, as is likely, this concept originates in a mythological context (the notion of the "primal man"), Paul has modified it to refer to the historical man Jesus. But as death is both past and present, resurrection is present only in Christ and is future for all whom he represents.

Just as in the Isaiah passage we have a forerunner of apocalyptic thought, so here we have a fragment of Christian apocalyptic which periodizes the future and assures the futurity of the resurrection of the dead. The scheme hinges on the future coming (Parousia) of Christ, the

The Resurrection of Our Lord

resurrection, the conquest of the spiritual powers—chief among them death—and the handing over of Christ's kingdom to the Father, with emphasis on the fact that the ultimate sovereignty is God's. The reign of Christ is present, however, having been inaugurated by his resurrection. Whatever the extent to which one can accept such an apocalyptic time scheme, one must acknowledge that it expresses an important dimension of Pauline thought—the notion that Christian life is not itself the realization of all that God has promised, but it is lived in the hope of the fullness of promise. Death remains a reality, but it is not ultimately final.

Gospel: Mark 16:1-8. The Gospel stories of the empty tomb most likely were not part of the earliest Christian proclamation of the resurrection (see, e.g., 1 Cor. 15:3-5), but, as the variations of them suggest, they proved to be an effective way to communicate resurrection faith. Mark may have used a traditional story, but it is the least clear of the four. It contains such implausible details as the intention of the women to anoint the body of Jesus, and such clearly Marcan additions as v. 7, which contains a sort of cross-reference to Mark 14:28. Despite all this, it remains a powerful story.

It is the more remarkable if indeed it was the intended ending of the Gospel of Mark (note that vv. 9-20 are not part of the original Gospel). Whether or not Mark knew any stories of resurrection appearances is uncertain. By ending his Gospel with this story, he ends on a double note of mystery, heightened by the women's reaction in v. 8, and of hope, expressed mainly in the promise of v. 7, which some think refers to the Parousia and others to a resurrection appearance. Such an ending is consistent with the Marcan emphasis on Jesus as the suffering, dying, rising Son of man with its explicit consequences for Christian discipleship understood as suffering with Christ in the hope of rising with him.

The empty tomb story of itself proves nothing: Matthew deals explicitly with this point in his discussion of the charge of stealing the body in 27:62-66 and 28:11-15, and Luke illustrates it in 24:22-24. The meaning of the empty tomb can only be revealed—and therefore accepted—only in faith. In the Marcan story the young man dressed in white very likely refers to an angel who interprets the empty tomb and thereby proclaims the Easter faith of the church: "He has risen, he is not here."

HOMILETICAL INTERPRETATION

The resurrection of Christ is the basis of Christian faith, and its liturgical celebration is the linchpin of the Christian year. Had there been no resurrection, the death of Jesus on the cross would have been, at most, the tragic death of a good man, like the death of Socrates. Because, beyond all expectation and reasonable hope, God raised him from the dead, his life and teaching were vindicated in spite of their bitter and even shameful end. More than that, humanity finds hope for its eternal life with God in this one man's conquest of mortality.

There are many different ways of looking at Easter. Consider at least the following two in preparing to preach on this most significant of all Christian feasts.

Easter represents God's conquest of the ultimate enemies of humanity. Human religions might be regarded as a variety of ways to deal with evil, or to celebrate the conquest of evil, which we humans cannot overcome by ourselves. Pagan agricultural religions celebrate the return of life every spring after the death of winter. The Jewish religion centers in the Exodus, the deliverance of God's people from slavery into Egypt by the crossing of the Red Sea. God's power is revealed not only in the conquest of winter and of all natural enemies but in the conquest of Eygpt and all historical foes.

The God of biblical faith reveals himself as Lord of nature and history. Yet the OT expresses the sense of all humanity in its recognition that evil nonetheless remains. Human life is still alienated and estranged from God by sin; death still cuts us off from communion with the Lord. "Dost thou work wonders for the dead? Do the shades rise up to praise thee? Is thy steadfast love declared in the grave, or thy faithfulness in Abaddon?" (Ps. 88:11–12). The Easter message is that in the resurrection of Christ from the dead the first disciples knew their sin (betraying Jesus) was forgiven and death was conquered in principle—"in power and beginning" (Tillich)—by his life beyond death.

The resurrection from the dead was hoped for by faithful Israelites. Had there not been expectation, the actuality of the resurrection would scarcely have been understood. But in postexilic Israel, as the actual state of affairs went from bad to worse, many who trusted in Yahweh began to see that he must vindicate himself *beyond* history, since history otherwise would be meaningless. The Pharisaic party expected the resurrection. The Sadducees did not. Apocalyptic literature looked for the general resurrection of the dead prior to the establishment of the kingdom of God in the last days. The Christian news is not that resurrection is a possiblity for human life—some people already longed for it. The Christian news is that in the resurrection of Christ the general resurrection has begun. The last days are at hand. The kingdom of God has been established "in principle."

The First Lesson, Isa. 25:6–9, is a vision of what the kingdom of God

The Resurrection of Our Lord

will look like. The Second Lesson, part of Paul's great excursus on the resurrection of the dead in 1 Corinthians 15, talks about the resurrection of Christ and the resurrection of "those who belong to Christ" (1 Cor. 15:23). The Gospel is the story of the announcement of the resurrection of Jesus to the three women who came early Easter morning to anoint his body. "He has risen, he is not here; see the place where they laid him" (Mark 16:6).

If one were to preach on all three texts, to help worshipers grasp the bearing of the service of the Word on the whole celebration, it might be useful to begin with the Gospel, the story of the original Easter experience. We encounter it in the Marcan version, since Cycle B is the year of Mark. As the exegesis points out, one of the striking features of the Marcan account of Easter morning is the abrupt, uncertain, even fearful conclusion: "Trembling and astonishment had come upon them; and they said nothing to anyone, for they were afraid" (Mark 16:8). Throughout the Scripture, God's revelations are awesome and inspire terror. In the face of them, one always has to be told to "fear not." The "young man in white" is certainly an indicator of divine revelation, communicating the meaning of the sight in the tomb. The sight in itself would prove nothing (see the exegesis). Nothing had prepared the earliest disciples for the resurrection of *one*. The apocalyptic hope was for a universal resurrection. The Gospel communicates a sense of the resurrection as a powerful mystery, which is perplexing and fearful. It can only be pondered and adored. Perhaps we must all begin our Easter celebration at this point.

The Second Lesson represents the reflection by the church's first great theologian, Paul, upon the meaning of the resurrection of Christ. Paul has to adjust the pre-Christian apocalyptic time scheme. The fathers, he concludes, were surely right in expecting a general resurrection, but they did not know that one man would be raised first. Paul uses the imagery of first fruits to make his case. Some of the harvest comes in first as the sure prelude to the whole. So one man, Christ, is raised from the dead as the sure beginning of the resurrection of "those who belong to Christ." Jesus' resurrection means that our resurrection has been assured, that sin and death have been conquered for us, and that God's rule over the whole of creation is now established—"in principle." By the Second Lesson we learn that the resurrection is *for us*.

The First Lesson is a beautiful description of what it will be like in God's kingdom. It is a vision of the fulfillment of human need and hope. We hear of a feast of food and drink—no hunger or thirst there. The veil cast over the nations will be destroyed. That verse is an enigmatic figure of speech, whose meaning is not at once apparent. One may interpret the phrase to mean that the hostility of nations which leads to war, plunder, famine, and holocaust will be once and forever destroyed, and the rich and fulfilling shalom for which the earth longs will prevail. Death will be swallowed up forever. "The last enemy to be destroyed is death" (1 Cor. 15:26).

This is the deliverance for which humanity has waited. In Christ it now has come. "Let us be glad and rejoice in his salvation" (Isa. 25:9).

First Lesson: Isa. 25:6-9. Preached on Easter Day, a sermon based on this text alone would assume the resurrection of Christ as its premise. Isaiah's vision would become the goal of resurrection life.

Such a sermon would have to wrestle with the relation between God's action and human initiative. The resurrection of Christ is the work of God, accomplished in spite of human hostility and opposition. Likewise, the fulfillment of the kingdom will take place, in God's time, as his work. The two phases, resurrection of Christ and the resurrection of those who are his, are related as first fruits and harvest.

What is the responsibility of Christians in the ever-lengthening meantime? By our history we will be found either in conformity and obedience to the will of God or in opposition to it. If the former, then surely the description of the kingdom in Isaiah is the charter for the world which those who live in hope seek to build here on earth—a life where want is removed, where peace and order reign among the nations of the world, and death is swallowed up.

Some attention must be given to what the swallowing up of death can mean. It is surely not enough to talk about the conquest of disease and the adding of years to the span of earthly existence. One cannot honestly proclaim, either, the end of dying. What one looks for, during the continuance of historical existence, is such a close relationship to God that one "abides in him"—to use Johannine language which later lessons in this season repeat—and in him enters eternal life (cf. 1 John 1:2-3). A Christian can know resurrection life now in faith, a life whose *quality* is eternal inasmuch as it is a life in God.

Second Lesson: 1 Cor. 15:19-28. Both the exegesis and the footnote in the RSV indicate the ambiguity in the Greek text of v. 19. The RSV prefers the translation, "If in this life we who are in Christ have only hope, we are of all men most to be pitied." The exegesis elects the alternative, "If in this life only we have hope, we are of all men most to be pitied."

The tension created by that ambiguity might be used to illuminate an important facet, or two important facets, of Easter faith. If the first reading is accepted, we understand that others—for example, pre-Christian apocalypticists or the Pharisees—might *hope* for the resurrection, but Christians have more than hope. Christ has *in fact* been raised. Resurrection is a present reality. If the Christian community is deceived about the reality of that aspect of its faith, indeed it is to be pitied. On the basis of the second reading, on the other hand, we understand that others, the whole world of well-intentioned humanity, might hope for a better life within the limits of this-worldly possibilities, but Christians hope not only for this life but also for the age to come. It is true that many modern Christians cannot share Paul's apocalyptic framework for the future of history. Many of us have to say that it is given to mortals not to know times and seasons but only the present grace of God. Yet if Christian faith gives us no more grounds for hope than the rest of well-intentioned humanity, we are of all people most to be pitied. Each of these versions communicates some of the truth of Easter. Is there a sermon there?

Gospel: Mark 16:1-8. In addition to the points already made about the Gospel reading—the announcement of the young man as the indicator of divine revelation, and the ending of the pericope on a note of fear—it is perhaps worth pointing out three other features of the narrative.

Like all resurrection accounts it is carefully dated "on the first day of the week." The First Day has replaced the Seventh Day as the holy day for the Christian community. This displacement of the Sabbath, most sacred of Jewish institutions, is a mark of the power and actuality of the resurrection. What would it take to make Christians shift our holy day away from Sunday?

There is no description of the resurrection, either in the Second Gospel or in any canonical account. What is described is the discovery, or the proclamation, of the resurrection, the first Christian kerygma: "He has risen, he is not here" (v. 6).

In this pericope of the Second Gospel there are no resurrection appearances. Disciples are told to go to Galilee, where they would see Jesus. If the text originally ended at v. 8 (see the exegesis), this Gospel would be evidence for the priority of Galilean encounters with the risen Lord. It is attractive to suppose that the Lord first appeared to his disciples when, in disappointment, they had returned to their workaday world and *there* discovered that the Lord was alive, had conquered death, and had commissioned them to preach the gospel to all the world.

Easter Evening or Easter Monday

Lutheran	Roman Catholic	Episcopal
Dan. 12:1c–3 or Jon. 2:2–9	Acts 2:14, 22–32	Acts 5:29a, 30–32 or Dan. 12:1–3
1 Cor. 5:6–8		1 Cor. 5:6b–8 or Acts 5:29a, 30–32
Luke 24:13–49	Matt. 28:8–15	Luke 24:13–35

EXEGESIS

First Lesson: Jon. 2:2–9. This beautiful and typical psalm of thanksgiving is embedded in the Book of Jonah, one of the most delightful didactic stories in the Bible. The psalm probably existed independently of the Jonah story to which it was later added. Jonah utters the prayer while in the belly of the fish. One might expect him to pray for rescue rather than thank God for a rescue already achieved: the ancient Greek translator of Jonah actually changed the tenses of some of the verbs. But in its setting in the book the fish is an instrument of deliverance, not itself the threat.

Expressed in the language of the Book of Psalms, the psalm is a fine example of thanksgiving for deliverance from danger of any kind. The image is a classic one: the endangered person being in Sheol, down in the pit, surrounded by the menacing waters, his cry being heard by God in the temple (see the prayer for help in Ps. 88 or the thanksgiving in Ps. 18:3–6). The reference to Sheol is metaphorical in such psalms: it does not mean literally that the psalmist has been raised from the dead. As the "sign of Jonah" in the Gospel tradition indicates, however, the early Christian interpretation of the psalm was more literal. The passage ends with a fundamental biblical notion, that deliverance comes from Yahweh himself.

Second Lesson: Acts 5:29a, 30–32. The early chapters of the Acts of the Apostles, which are drawn upon heavily in the lectionary of the Easter season, contain several summaries of the early Christian preaching in forms that generally reflect Luke's own understanding of the gospel message. The brief summary in our pericope is spoken before the Sanhedrin in an interrogation following the apostles' miraculous escape from prison. It is a typical summary, and in the form used in the lectionary it is not notably dependent on its context.

The contents of the summary are quite characteristic of the kerygma of Acts, which is never merely repeated verbatim but always varied. Its stages are death, resurrection, exaltation, witnessing, the gift of the Holy Spirit, repentance, and forgiveness of sins (cf. Luke 24:46-49). Using the language of Deut. 21:22-23 ("hanging on a tree"), which greatly heightens the horror of the crucifixion, Luke typically confronts the hostile Jewish authorities with responsibility for the death of Jesus. In connection with kerygmatic statements about the exaltation of Jesus, often with a quotation from Ps. 110:1 (as in Acts 2:34-35) or an allusion to it (as here), Luke varies the titles predicated of the exalted one. In Acts 2:36 we find "Lord and Christ" (Messiah), here "Leader and Savior." The title that is correctly translated "Leader" (Greek *archēgos*) is very rare in the NT and is puzzling when used without a modifier. It may be best to understand it as "Leader to (new) life," as in Acts 3:15 (where it is sometimes wrongly translated "Author of life"). In this case the word forms an appropriate pair with the Hellenistic title "Savior." The soteriology of repentance and forgiveness of sins is distinctively Lucan (again see Luke 24:47). In Luke-Acts there are no notions of redemption, reconciliation, sacrifice, etc., such as we find in Paul or Hebrews, for example. It is the preaching of the kerygma that affords an opportunity for the human response of repentance and the divine response of forgiveness. The role of the apostles (later in Acts the role of Paul also) is to be witnesses who proclaim "these things" (see Luke 24:48; Acts 1:8, 22; 22:15; etc.). It is the gift of God's Spirit that empowers the apostles to fulfill this role (Luke 24:49; Acts 1:8), so that the Holy Spirit may be thought of as a co-witness.

Gospel: Luke 24:13-35. Some of the best-told stories in the Gospels are resurrection appearance stories. One thinks of Jesus' appearance to Mary Magdalene in John 20:11-18 and, of course, of the Emmaus story. This beloved narrative is actually a complex one in its present form, incorporating some clearly Lucan redactional additions and many themes of the resurrection tradition. For example, the reference to the empty tomb story in 24:21b-24 interrupts the narrative somewhat and serves to link it with the preceding story in 24:1-11. Similarly, the report of his prior appearance to Simon (Peter) in v. 34 (or even the whole return to Jerusalem in vv. 33-35) is quite extraneous to the story and was doubtless added by Luke because of the tradition that the risen Lord first appeared to Peter (see 1 Cor. 15:5). In view of the prominence of Peter in the opening chapters of Acts, Luke might be expected to have an interest in such a tradition, even though he has no story of an appearance to Peter. One should not conclude, however, that what remains is merely a traditional story handed on by Luke. Whatever its origin, it is written in Lucan style and contains some of Luke's theological themes. For example, vv. 19-20, concerning the work and death of Jesus, are very much in the style of the early Christian kerygma repeated in Acts, for the formulation of which Luke himself was responsible.

The risen Christ's emphasis on the necessity of his suffering (v. 26) is an important Lucan theme. One of Luke's underlying theological motifs is the concept of a salvation history, which links the past of Israel to the time of Christ and the Christian church via the notion of promise (in the Scriptures) and fulfillment (in the events of the Gospel and Acts). This notion is explicitly introduced in Jesus' first public appearance in Luke 4:16-30 and is often repeated thereafter in both of Luke's works.

The recognition scene in the Emmaus story takes place "in the breaking of the bread," which inevitably reminds both the ancient and the modern reader of the Lord's Supper. In fact, the language of Christ's actions in v. 30 is eucharistic language (cf. Luke 22:19 and also 9:16) in which, despite variants reflecting different eucharistic traditions in the early church, there is a recognizable constancy. On the level of the appearance story, the disciples recognize Jesus as they knew him at the Last Supper. But on another level, Luke doubtless wants to suggest that it is in the worship life of the Christian communities that the risen Christ may be encountered.

The location of Emmaus has fascinated Christians for centuries. Four different places in the environs of Jerusalem have been suggested either by tradition or by modern scholarship. The problem is insoluble, but what is more important, it may also be quite irrelevant to Luke's purposes in dramatizing so skillfully the early Christian experience of the risen Lord.

HOMILETICAL INTERPRETATION

These three lections are tied together only loosely, by their common illumination of the resurrection of Christ.

The OT lesson is a psalm of thanksgiving for deliverance by the hand of God from some great danger. References to Sheol and to "the waters [which] closed in over me and the deep . . . round about me" (Jon. 2:5) were figurative expressions of the psalmist's distress. The author of Jonah used the psalm to refer to Jonah's particular plight "in the belly of the fish." NT writers understood the sign of Jonah as a sign of the resurrection (Matt. 12:39-40; 16:4) and interpreted the psalm to apply to Jesus' deliverance from the realm of the dead. In any case, "deliverance belongs to the Lord" (Jon. 2:9). That confession of faith is true in general; if in Christ, believing Christians find deliverance from the power of death itself, the last enemy, this new experience of God's deliverance lends new appreciation to God's power to save in every situation.

The Second Lesson is an early proclamation of God's deliverance of Jesus. "The God of our fathers" (who delivered Israel from Egypt, Jonah from the belly of the fish, and many others from great perils) has "raised Jesus. . . . God exalted him at his right hand as Leader and Savior" (vv. 30-31). (See the note in the exegesis on "Leader.") Resurrection means to believers not only hope beyond death but also repentance and forgiveness of sins now (v. 31). E. Schillebeeckx, in his book *Jesus*, makes a strong case for understanding the original experience of resurrection as when Peter and the other apostles experienced Jesus' forgiveness for their denial and desertion of him—a dead man cannot forgive sins. (Cf. Edward Schillebeeckx, *Jesus* [New York: Seabury Press, 1979], pp. 390-92.)

The Gospel is an account of one of the first appearances of Jesus after his resurrection. This appearance occurred on Easter afternoon, "in the breaking of the bread." As the exegesis points out, Luke probably wanted to suggest that "it is in the worship life of the Christian communities that the risen Christ may be encountered," then as now. One of the places where resurrection becomes actual for us is in the Eucharist, which includes—now as then—both an interpretation of the Word of God and a celebration of the Supper.

First Lesson: Jon. 2:2-9. There is ordinarily little homiletical problem in persuading a congregation of the reality of evil. In family life, under economic pressure, and among contending nations situations abound in which we can easily imagine ourselves as being "cast into the deep, into the heart of the seas, and the flood was round about me; all thy waves and billows passed over me" (v. 3). It seems likely that the author of Jonah meant this image to be understood as a reference to the woes of Israel in the postexilic years, when it was written. We can make the same reference for our time.

Unlike our text, we would doubtless find it both unprofitable and incorrect simply to make God the cause of our troubles. It is not so easy to say "*Thou* didst cast me into the deep." How are we to understand the origin of evil? It is an impenetrable mystery. On the one hand, we should not ascribe evil to a source independent of God. Christianity is not a dualistic religion. The source of evil is under God's control. On the other hand, we should be wary of making evil God's precisely measured recompense for each of our disobedient acts and thoughts. We can come up with no neatly graduated scale of evil in proportion to human sin. Evil seems to be the net result of freedom misused; each act of human arrogance is met by an overreaction from the victim of that arrogance, the whole proceeding in a mounting, incalculable, and disorderly spiral, altogether out of human control. There is no rationality to the fate of Israel, as the book of Job is designed to show, or to human fate, as the cross clearly tells Christians. Yet Easter faith is the joyful discovery that what is beyond human understanding and control is nevertheless in some unimaginable way a creature of God and under his control. However irrational and devastating evil may be, its agents are still the servants of God (though rebellious servants) and in the end "Deliverance belongs to the Lord!" even over sin, death, and hell.

Second Lesson: Acts 5:29a, 30-32. In addition to the two points we have already made about this text—God's raising and exalting of Jesus and the recognition of him as Messiah (Leader and Savior), and the relation between resurrection on the one hand and repentance and forgiveness on the other—the third element which needs to be noted is the witness of the Christian community: "And we are witnesses to these things, and so is the Holy Spirit whom God has given to those who obey him."

The experience of forgiveness and deliverance from sin is so powerful that it impels those who receive it to communicate their great good fortune. Christians are filled with the Holy Spirit. The gift of the Spirit accompanies the resurrection. That Spirit "bears witness with our spirits" (Rom. 8:16) that God has delivered us from the final evil. Such witness is inseparable from the Easter message; it accounts for the continuance of the Christian community in the power of the Spirit, and it devolves upon us today as heirs of the resurrection.

Gospel: Luke 24:13-35. There are two kinds of testimony to the resurrection of the Lord: the narratives of Easter morning in each of the four Gospels, proclaiming the resurrection as an event which has already occurred—"He has risen, he is not here" (Mark 16:6); and the accounts of the resurrection as experienced by disciples, such as this Easter afternoon encounter of the two disciples with the risen Lord "in

Easter Evening or Easter Monday

the breaking of the bread" (v. 35). The first is ineffable and can only be uttered in awe and fear. The second has been the constitutive element of the life of the church from Easter until the present. On Easter morning the preacher must deal with the former. The appointed Gospel for Easter Monday allows the preacher to deal with the latter.

The elements of the story are suggestive of the Christian Eucharist. It is striking to note how many of the appearances of the risen Lord recorded in the NT occur at meals. The first part of the narrative concerns the events of Good Friday and Easter morning—the disappointment and discouragement of the Christian group in the face of their leader's death, and their perplexity at what the women encountered on Easter morning when they went to the tomb. This attitude toward the discovery of the tomb agrees with what we heard from Mark at the morning service.

What ensues in the Lucan pericope is a reinterpretation of scripture by the unknown guest. The events of Good Friday and Easter can be understood as the fulfillment of God's dealings with his people if the ancient scriptures are interpreted in the light of these events. Moses and the prophets (a phrase used to designate the whole Scripture of the Old Covenant) must be regarded afresh in the light of Christ, and it is Christ himself—in our day Christ through his Spirit—who opens to us this level of meaning. To encounter the risen Lord requires a "breaking open of the Scripture" (in the old evangelical phrase) so that disciples' hearts burn within us (v. 32), prior to a recognition of the Lord.

But then there is a meal, reminiscent of the Last Supper, where disciples were told to "Do this in remembrance of me" (in one version of Luke [Luke 22:19mg.] and in Paul [1 Cor. 11:24–25]). In this mealtime setting the Lord makes himself known. He was truly present for Cleopas and his companion, as he is truly present for us. Eucharist is an experience of resurrection which Christians today can wonderingly and thankfully share.

It is surely true to Christian eucharistic experience through the ages that even as the disciples' eyes were opened and they recognized him, "he vanished out of their sight" (v. 31).

The Second Sunday of Easter

Lutheran	Roman Catholic	Episcopal	Pres/UCC/Chr	Meth/COCU
Acts 3:13–15, 17–26	Acts 4:32–35	Acts 3:12a, 13–15, 17–26 or Isa. 26:2–9, 19	Acts 4:32–35	Acts 3:12a, 13–15, 17–26 or Isa. 26:2–9, 19
1 John 5:1–6	1 John 5:1–6	1 John 5:1–6 or Acts 3:12a, 13–15, 17–26	1 John 5:1–6	1 John 5:1–6
John 20:19–31	John 20:19–31	John 20:19–31	Matt. 28:11–20	John 20:19–31

EXEGESIS

First Lesson: Acts 3:13–15, 17–26. This kerygmatic sermon of Peter has its setting near the temple at Jerusalem just after Peter and John have healed—or rather, served as the instruments for God's healing of—a man lame from birth. When the lectionary omits v. 16, which is textually confused in any case, it means to give the sermon a more universal significance, which it readily can have. The sermon is an example of the Christian preaching to Jews, like the similar speeches in the early chapters of Acts. The statement that God—identified in typically Jewish, or biblical, fashion—has glorified Jesus is at once a reference to Isa. 52:13 and an explanation of the healing "in the name of Jesus Christ of Nazareth" (v. 6).

It has often been claimed that this sermon, unlike others in Acts, represents the earliest preaching of the primitive church because of its archaic language and its Christology. But it is also possible, and perhaps more likely, that Luke is merely using archaizing and very "Jewish" language to vary the pattern of the preaching and to connote a period of preaching that is far in the past from his vantage point. In fact, apart from the archaizing, apocalyptic language, the sermon contains many typically Lucan features and no ideas that are incompatible with Luke's own theology. Some of the typically Lucan elements are the following: the Jews' responsibility for the death of Jesus, which is tempered by the motif of ignorance in v. 17 (the audience not being a hostile one as in Acts 5:30–32); the resurrection; the theme of prophetic promise and fulfillment; the soteriology of repentance and forgiveness of sins; and the indefinite expectation of a future coming of Jesus in his messianic role. With regard to the last point, it is actually characteristic of the view presented in Acts that Jesus is to return as Messiah (having been so designated by his resurrection and exaltation) but at an indefinite time in the future—in apocalyptic language "times of refreshing" or "the time for establishing all."

Several important aspects of Lucan Christology are reflected in the titles given to Jesus in this passage. First, he is called God's "servant." The word can also mean simply "child," but in view of the explicit use of the servant song of Isaiah 53 in Acts 8:32-33, the reference is undoubtedly to an application of the servant passages to Christ. The emphasis is not on the servant as suffering, however, but on the servant as glorified or exalted. Second, in addition to the messianic title "Holy and Righteous One," Jesus is called "Leader to (new) life" (not "Author of life" as in the RSV). The allusion here is to the resurrection, which implies the future resurrection of Jesus' followers. Third, by explicitly, though selectively, quoting Deut. 18:15-19, Luke identifies Jesus as the eschatological prophet foretold by Moses, thus reinforcing his view of the continuity of the Christian dispensation with the history of Israel. (Note that "raise up" in v. 22 does not refer to the resurrection of Jesus but simply means "bring into being," as in Deut. 18:15.)

Second Lesson: 1 John 5:1-6. As we approach a series of readings from the First Epistle of John, as well as from the Gospel of John, it is important to be aware of the relationship between the two documents. The question still is a controversial one, and we can do no more here than state a position briefly. In the view of an increasing number of interpreters, we are dealing with two different authors, who come from the same Johannine church and therefore share a great deal of distinctive religious language without necessarily understanding all of it the same way. The Epistle very likely was written after the Gospel and, in part, to deal with a tragic division in the Johannine church occasioned by differing interpretations of the Gospel itself.

The central issue, as our pericope makes clear, is Christology. What do those who follow Jesus believe about him? For the faith that overcomes the "world" (the realm of those who reject Jesus) is faith in Jesus. Three things are asserted: true children of God believe that Jesus is the Christ (Messiah), though the implications of this title are not spelled out; Jesus is the Son of God; and Jesus came by water and blood. The symbolism of water and blood is best understood here as referring to the baptism of Jesus (although this is not narrated but at best alluded to in the Fourth Gospel) and to his death—that is, to his true humanity, encompassed in the Gospel message between these two poles. As v. 6 suggests, there may have been some Johannine Christians who denied the real humanity of Jesus by denying the reality of his death, without necessarily objecting to the baptism. If so, they cannot appeal to an inspiration of God's Spirit because it is to the full humanity of Jesus that the Spirit bears witness. Those who have such faith are those who fulfill the commandment of love of one another, which is central to the Fourth Gospel.

Gospel: John 20:19-31. The Fourth Gospel's account of two appearances of the risen Jesus to his disciples brings to a conclusion several important themes of the Gospel, many of them prefigured in the Farewell Discourses (John 13—17). The latter include, for example, the coming of Jesus (14:18), the greeting of peace (14:27), joy (16:20-22), seeing the Lord (16:16-19), sending the disciples (17:18), receiving the Holy Spirit (14:26), and dealing with sin (16:8-9). What is conspicuously absent in this passage is any emphasis on the resurrection of Jesus. Jesus' identity is in question as is his relationship to his disciples, but the resurrection is not at the heart of the Johannine gospel message.

Stories of resurrection appearances to the disciples in the Gospel tradition are also stories of commissioning (see Matt. 28:18-20; Luke 24:47), and this is true of the first appearance story here. Three aspects of the commission are important. First, the disciples are sent as the Father has sent Jesus; in consequence, the mission of the disciples is to be in continuity with the mission of Jesus. Second, Jesus confers the Holy Spirit, promised repeatedly as the Paraclete in the Farewell Discourses, who will enable the disciples to undertake the mission. Though he lacks the elaborate time scheme of Pentecost in Acts, the Fourth Evangelist shares much with Luke regarding the role of the Spirit. Third, the specific commission is phrased in terms of what must have been a traditional saying dealing with church order, of forgiving and retaining sins (cf. Matt. 18:18). But how does the Fourth Gospel understand the saying? If one traces the concept of sin or sins (singular and plural are interchangeable as John 8:21-24 shows) in this Gospel, it becomes apparent that sin is the refusal to believe (see, e.g., 16:8-9). Thus the disciples' mission is to continue Jesus' mission by confronting people with the option either to believe that Jesus is the Christ, the Son of God, or to remain hardened in unbelief.

The disciples, however, have the task of offering faith to those who have not seen, and the Thomas incident serves to ground such faith in a beatitude of the risen Jesus. Thomas does not merely doubt; he sets up his own conditions for believing, which suggest the kind of faith based merely on signs that Jesus has repeatedly rejected (see, e.g., 4:48). It is not said that Thomas's conditions are fulfilled. Instead he affirms a lofty christological faith, because he has seen. There will be those who do not see but have only the written Gospel in which to encounter Jesus.

HOMILETICAL INTERPRETATION

First Lesson: Acts 3:13–15; 17–26. If one were to preach on this lesson alone, one might invite the congregation to consider God's strange dealings with his people: the call of Abraham with the corollary of the mission to the world (Gen. 12:3; 17:5; 22:18; Acts 3:25), the sending of Jesus as Leader to life (Acts 3:15; 5:31; see the exegesis), Jesus' rejection, God's vindication and exaltation of him, the witness of the believing community, and the summons to repentance and forgiveness while history continues (v. 21).

Most of these points have been discussed already in the homiletical interpretation for Easter Monday. The new emphasis in this reading is the continuity between the Old and New Covenants. The work of Christ is the fulfillment of the hopes of Israel. What had been expected has now come to pass, although not in the way in which it was expected. God is full of surprises.

The preacher would be well advised to generalize as much as possible on the theme of expectation and fulfillment. It is not simply that Jesus fulfills OT prophecy in a surprising way; he does that, and the reinterpretation of prophecy—in such a way that this fulfillment becomes plain—is a crucial part of the Easter message. Yet Jesus also fulfills primal human expectation. The dream of peace and freedom from want and the hope for the conquest of death and the world (1 John 5:5) are not merely Jewish but essentially human. It continues to be true that God fulfills human expectations in strange ways.

The preacher would especially want to generalize the element of the Jewish rejection of Jesus as the Christ. Passages like Acts 3:14–15 lend color to the charge that the NT is an anti-Semitic book. The preacher has a special responsibility in our time to make clear that the rejection of Christ is not merely an event which once occurred in Jewish history, but most significantly, it is a universal and continual human problem. All God's people, especially the church, are tempted to repudiate the new duties which new occasions require of believers in Christ.

Second Lesson: 1 John 5:1–6. The point of hearing this lesson on this Sunday is to underline the importance and nature of belief in Jesus as the Christ; it serves as a companion piece to the Gospel reading.

Faith makes the believer a child of God: "To all who received him, who believed in his name, he gave power to become children of God; who were born, not of blood nor of the will of the flesh nor of the will of men, but of God" (John 1:12–13; the plural form of this text is preferable and crucial). By faith we are *all* children of God. Here, as always in the

NT, faith means not only subscription to doctrines (belief that certain things are true) but trust and reliance on the saving power of Christ (faith in the person of Christ and in God, his Father and ours). One stakes one's life on Christ. One risks life in order to find it. One is willing to do so because of the Easter message of resurrection, new life, and forgiveness. In Christ, the only Son, we all become children.

Children love parents and each other, and love involves obedience (vv. 1–2). But obedience does not earn love, here or elsewhere in the NT. There is no justification by works. On the other hand, there is no faith worthy of the name which does not result in works of love for others. The ethical component of faith is notable in 1 John; this theme will be developed further in the section for the Fourth Sunday of Easter.

Faith overcomes the world. The world, rebellious and hostile to God—as always in Johannine literature—is hostile to us also. Few members of a congregation will be unable to recognize this dimension of the reality of their lives. The Easter message is that faith overcomes the hostile world *for us*.

As we have already indicated, such faith does not require physical seeing, for Jesus comes not only in the flesh but also in water and blood, baptism and Eucharist (v. 6).

Gospel: John 20:19–31. This reading continues the narrative of events on the first Easter Day. Now it is evening and the disciples are gathered in Jerusalem, presumably for the evening meal. Jesus appears. Dare we suggest a eucharistic appearance? At the very least, the preacher will be able to appeal to the congregation's eucharistic experience as a point of contact.

This passage falls into two parts which do not seem to constitute a unity. The preacher who uses this text should probably select one or the other, since both are so rich. One is the breathing of the Spirit upon the disciples; here is the story of Pentecost for the Fourth Evangelist. The second is the appearance to Thomas and the blessing of those who have not seen and yet believe.

The risen Lord imparts the Holy Spirit to the disciples. Life in the resurrection is life in the Spirit, now known as the Spirit of the incarnate One. So closely related are these aspects of Christian experience that the resurrection and the coming of the Spirit are represented here as occurring on the same day; and the earliest celebration of Pascha, the Christian Passover, preserved this unity.

The risen Lord brings peace (v. 19). In place of the awe and terror with which the women left the tomb, the Lord announces shalom, the "Fear not" with which the God of biblical faith accompanies his numinous appearances. Peace is intended in the largest context. In place of the disruption of the created order and the alienation between God and humanity entailed by sin, now there is peace. Death, which came into the world on account of sin, has been vanquished "in principle" in the resurrection of Christ. Sin is forgiven.

It is an important psychological fact that sin has to be forgiven by someone. Hence the apostolic band is empowered not only to proclaim forgiveness in the abstract, as they do in the speeches in Acts, but to forgive in God's name. Forgiveness is administered in the church. Every church finds some way to make gospel forgiveness actual through its ministry, for the actuality of forgiveness is the actuality of eternal life. "We know that we have passed out of death into life because we love the brethren" (1 John 3:14).

Perhaps the most obvious sermon suggested by the provision of lessons for this day would be a sermon on Easter faith. It might be entitled "Ways to Faith." One could develop the way of *seeing*—Thomas's way; the way of *tradition*—the way of responding to the witness of those who have seen (here one might point out the repeated references in the Easter lessons from Acts to being witnesses of the resurrection: Acts 1:22; 5:32; 3:15; etc.); and the way of *sacramental participation*—the way of appropriating the Christ who comes by "water and blood," baptism and Eucharist.

If one were to construct a sermon like this, it would be important not to downgrade Thomas as faithless. That move has been made so universally that it has even given us the phrase "doubting Thomas," although the words are not in the passage. Not even the implication of faithlessness is in the passage. Thomas is blessed with the same word that Jesus used to bless those who do not see.

Thomas was one of the Twelve (v. 24). He wanted what the other members of the Twelve had already received—a direct experience of the risen Lord. As we shall discover on the Seventh Sunday of Easter, that was one of the conditions imposed on the successor to Judas. For the Twelve witnessed to the resurrection in a unique way (see the discussion on the First Lesson for Easter 7). They knew Jesus in the flesh. It was crucial at the beginning of the Christian movement that there should have been eyewitnesses to the resurrection. Christian faith is based on historical event.

But with the passing of the first generation, this witness became impossible. Ongoing generations cannot have the experience which the Twelve had. They cannot see in the sense that the Twelve saw. However, there are other ways to faith: through the continuing witness to the Easter message and through direct sacramental participation—through a ministry of Word and Sacrament, we might say. Also, as the reading from 1 John makes explicit, the way to faith is opened by love for one's neighbor and obedience to the commandments of God (1 John 5:1-2; cf. below, the homiletical interpretation for Easter 4 and Easter 5). All these are necessary ways to faith.

The Third Sunday of Easter

Lutheran	Roman Catholic	Episcopal	Pres/UCC/Chr	Meth/COCU
Acts 4:8-12	Acts 3:13-15, 17-19	Acts 4:5-12 or Mic. 4:1-5	Acts 3:13-15, 17-19	Acts 4:5-12 or Mic. 4:1-5
1 John 1:1—2:2	1 John 2:1-5a	1 John 1:1—2:2 or Acts 4:5-12	1 John 2:1-6	1 John 1:1—2:6
Luke 24:36-49	Luke 24:35-48	Luke 24:36b-48	Luke 24:36-49	Luke 24:35-49

EXEGESIS

First Lesson: Acts 4:5-12. Having healed a man lame from birth, preached the gospel to the crowd of Jewish witnesses, and been arrested by the temple authorities, Peter and John then appear before the Sanhedrin to account for their actions. The assembly is rather solemnly described but not with a concern for historical accuracy. Annas is no longer the high priest; Caiaphas is. John and Alexander are otherwise unknown to us. Most of all, the question put to the apostles in v. 7 is much more a literary introduction to Peter's reply than a plausible Jewish interrogation, especially in the context of 4:1-4. Peter responds "filled with the Holy Spirit." Throughout Acts it is the Holy Spirit that empowers and emboldens the Christians both to defend themselves and to carry out their mission. But there is more here. This is one of Luke's many allusions to his Gospel which serve to emphasize the ongoing continuity of salvation history. The reference is to Jesus' instruction to the disciples in Luke 12:11-12: "And when they bring you before the synagogues and the rulers and the authorities, do not be anxious how or what you are to answer or what you are to say; for the Holy Spirit will teach you in that very hour what you ought to say."

Peter's speech includes a very brief summary of the essential elements of the kerygma in v. 10, and in v. 11 it makes use of one of the early adaptations of an OT text to Jesus: Ps. 118:22 (the introductory pronoun, "this" in the RSV, should be understood as a reference to Jesus himself in v. 10). This passage is used of Jesus, in its Septuagint form, in Mark 12:10-11 and its parallels and also in 1 Pet. 2:7. Here in Acts the passage is recognizably the same, but the language is notably different, suggesting that it may have circulated in early Christian churches in more than one form. Luke's editorial contribution is to add the words "by you," thus heightening the theme of the rejection of Jesus by the Jewish authorities—in a speech delivered before a hostile audience of these authorities. The image of the stone that has become the "head of the corner" is not entirely clear. Many interpreters have espoused the view that this is not a cornerstone but the capstone of a vault that holds the building together.

The healing and saving (the same word in Greek) power of the name of Jesus is a significant theme for Luke. While it undoubtedly connotes the quasi-magical power of the name of a deity in miracle working, for Luke it refers to the continuing presence of Jesus at work in the world through the invocation of his name on the part of his followers.

Second Lesson: 1 John 1:1—2:6. As one approaches the opening passages of the First Epistle of John, one is struck by two things: the use of language familiar from the Fourth Gospel and the introduction of some very non-Johannine language. What characterizes the former is the difference in the meaning of familiar expressions. For example, in 1 John 1:1-4 (often called the Prologue to the Epistle because it seems to be modeled on the Prologue to the Gospel) the emphasis is on "the word of life," but this expression seems to mean the gospel message about Jesus rather than the Word as a designation of the preexistent Son of God. The author of the Epistle affirms his personal witness to this word from the beginning of its proclamation in the Johannine community. Second, one notes the language of light and of darkness, familiar from both Jewish and Hellenistic religious circles. But whereas in the Gospel it is Jesus who is the light of the world (John 8:12), here "God is light and in him is no darkness at all." Not only is the focus more theocentric but the imagery is even more ethically oriented than in the Gospel. Third, sin is a major issue in this passage (and throughout the Epistle), but sin is not restricted in meaning to the refusal to believe; it seems to be used in its more general meaning of any moral transgression. Sin is not the final rejection of Jesus that it appears to be in the Gospel, but thanks to the "advocate," or Paraclete, Jesus, it can be forgiven.

The most striking "new" language in this Johannine context is found in the traditional soteriological expressions. Well known from other parts of the NT, they are completely absent from the Fourth Gospel: "the blood of Jesus his Son cleanses us from all sin," "he is the expiation for our sins," and similar expressions. These phrases suggest an attempt on the part of the author to assimilate the traditional Johannine soteriology of revelation with a more traditional Christian view of atonement. Equally foreign to the language of the Fourth Gospel is the emphasis on "fellowship," both with one another and with the Father and his Son. The Epistle is very conscious of the fact that a proper profession of faith in Christ and God is a life according to the truth, which manifests itself in genuine community—a community that has been broken, as the Epistle goes on to lament. In the Gospel Jesus had proclaimed: "By this all will know that you are my disciples, if you have love for one another" (John 13:35). The Epistle makes Jesus' love command a central criterion for Christian community.

Gospel: Luke 24:35-49. Through the repetition of v. 35 in the lectionary, this Gospel passage shows its link to the Emmaus story read on Easter evening. In this part of Luke's Gospel we have to choose between a longer and a shorter text, that is, whether or not to include v. 40. Though the choice in some other cases is important for understanding Luke, in our pericope the variants do not materially affect the meaning.

In Luke's Gospel the appearance to the Eleven has two main foci, the reality of the risen Jesus and the commissioning of the apostles. As for the first, Luke is at much greater pains than the other evangelists (and quite the opposite of Paul, who insists on the spiritual character of the risen body) to emphasize the physical reality of the risen Jesus. The Eleven react in fright, as though seeing a ghost. This detail corresponds to the larger theme of failure to recognize the risen Lord (as in the Emmaus story) or even of doubt (as in Matt 28:17). To dispel the impression, Jesus not only invites the Eleven to touch him (compare John 20:27) but eats a meal in their presence. The fact that he is offered a meal of fish is generally thought to reflect the origin of the appearance story in a Galilean tradition (as in John 21). Luke makes it a Jerusalem appearance to fit his theological-geographical scheme of the progression of the Christian message from Galilee to the center of Judaism, Jerusalem, and eventually (in Acts) on to Rome. The Christian movement derives its power from God himself; there is no turning back. The geographical point is explicit in vv. 47-48, especially if we read "beginning from Jerusalem" with v. 48 (the problem is a textual one and is difficult to decide on textual grounds alone).

The Easter message of Jesus is even more significant for Luke because it summarizes several major themes of his theology which we have already seen in various passages of Acts. These include the fulfillment of biblical promise, the soteriology of repentance and forgiveness of sins, the role of the apostles as witnesses, and the promise of the Holy Spirit ("power from on high"). Jesus' words actually serve as a programmatic statement for Luke's second volume, especially the reminder that the message is to be preached "to all nations" (v. 47).

HOMILETICAL INTERPRETATION

First Lesson: Acts 4:5-12. This pericope purports to be Peter's speech to the Sanhedrin (see the exegesis), before which he and John were taken for teaching the people about Jesus and the resurrection. Filled with the Holy Spirit, Peter proclaims the rejection of Jesus by the rulers of Israel and God's raising of him from the dead. By the power of the risen Jesus, the lame man had been healed. Once again we find that life in the resurrection and life in the Spirit are virtually synonymous.

If preachers have not yet used the opportunity provided by earlier lections to remind their congregations of the need to witness, to give an account of the faith that is in them, perhaps this could be a good occasion to do so. That Christians should have a canned spiel which they turn on at the slightest provocation is not at all what these Easter passages have in mind. Such witnessing is a travesty of what the NT describes. Christians should not be intimidated by the power, sophistication, or apathy of nonbelievers; and when given an opportunity, as Peter was by that priestly gathering (v. 7), they should take their life in their hands and, without carefully figuring out ahead of time what would be "relevant" or "tactful," trust the Holy Spirit to find the right words (cf. Mark 13:11). It would be a useful homiletical endeavor, sometime during this season of witness and mission, to wrestle with the difference between effective and ineffective ways for lay persons to testify to the significance of their faith. A few people, perhaps, need to be discouraged from frequent, insensitive, and mechanical speechmaking, which only feeds their own egos. Many, many more need to be encouraged to articulate what life in Christ and life in the Spirit means to them.

The new element in this pericope, absent in the earlier lessons from Acts we have examined, is the relation of proclamation to a healing, to a "mighty work." A healing also occurred in connection with last week's First Lesson, it will be remembered, but for several reasons the one verse which alluded to it was omitted from the lectionary version. This week the reference is unmistakable and unavoidable. In fact, the resurrection of Christ and the coming of the Spirit are attended by "signs and wonders" (see Easter 4). The narratives in Acts are ful   healings, speaking in tongues (2:4; 10:46; etc.), miraculo   nces (12:6–11; 16:25–34), exorcisms (19:13), visions (10:   tions (9:4). 1 Corinthians 12—13 expands the list of gifts of the   clude what modern congregations might regard as more or   ormal ways, culminating in the greatest of the gifts, agape (1 C   ife in the resurrection, or life in the Spirit, in any case,   lpable difference to the believer. One does not believe in or   ve the gift, but one does not truly live in the Spirit without re   e gift. Whether ordinary or extraordinary, it is always note   makes us humbly thankful.

Second Lesson: 1 John 1:1—2:6. An absolutely tight relationship is here established between fellowship with God, which is eternal life, and fellowship with one's neighbor. To claim the former and yet fail to manifest the latter is to live a lie. The point is as elemental and plain now as it was then, and the temptation to cloak arrogance and contempt for others in the robes of righteousness and religion is as seductive now as then.

The verses also contain a winsome and deceptively simple statement of Jesus' power to cleanse us from all sin and the continuation of Christian believers in sin. The preacher might profitably explore the paradox. "The blood of Jesus his Son cleanses us from all sin" (v. 7, 9); Christians are therefore free from sin. On the other hand, the perennial testimony of the most devout and sensitive Christian spirits is that they—and all of us—continue in sin. We are not free from its grip. "If we say we have no sin, we deceive ourselves and the truth is not in us" (v. 8). Christians must not be presumptuous and arrogant on the assumption that they have been forgiven and made righteous. Sin always threatens. On the other hand, Christians must not be complacent and cynical about their sins, in the expectation that forgiveness is always available. "God will forgive," Voltaire once announced, "it is his business" (*C'est son métier*). Christian life is a humble and grateful acceptance of forgiveness, freely tendered, and also perpetual striving to be righteous and to be obedient to the will of God in thanksgiving for all that he has done for us. Those two aspects of Christian consciousness exist side by side, the tension between them resolved only in the higher power and mercy of God himself.

The passage also contains a ringing affirmation of the worldwide relevance of Christ's atoning death. "He is the expiation for our sins, and not for ours only, but also for the sins of the whole world" (2:2). We cannot cling to Christ as a private possession. To hold the gospel close, in miserly fashion, is to lose it. To offer it to the world is to claim it as our own. The universality of the Christian mission is also a theme of the Gospel for today and other lections of the Easter season. Universality of mission is not quite the same thing as universality of salvation, which the Christian tradition has never quite been able to affirm. But it is clearly true that no finite mortal should dare to judge whom God saves and whom he rejects. The church is commissioned to offer the good news of God's forgiveness and of his conquest of death to everyone. Do we in our day accept that charge?

Gospel: Luke 24:35-49. This pericope, like last week's Gospel, establishes the special ministry of the Twelve as those who "saw" the resurrection in some unusually immediate, if to us altogether unimaginable, way (Luke 24:39, 42; cf. John 20:20, and of course the whole Thomas story). Material for the development of this point will be found in the Gospel discussion for the Second Sunday of Easter and the Second Lesson for the Seventh Sunday of Easter.

Other motifs in this pericope have also appeared in other lessons and have been discussed in other places in this volume: the reinterpretation of OT Scripture, the connection between resurrection and repentance and forgiveness, the charge to bear witness and pursue the mission, the promise of the Spirit, and the ascension of the Lord.

The Fourth Sunday of Easter

Lutheran	Roman Catholic	Episcopal	Pres/UCC/Chr	Meth/COCU
Acts 4:23-33	Acts 4:8-12	Acts 4:(23-31) 32-37 or Ezek. 34:1-10	Acts 4:8-12	Acts 4:23-37 or Ezek. 34:1-10
1 John 3:1-2	1 John 3:1-2	1 John 3:1-8 or Acts 4:(23-31) 32-37	1 John 3:1-3	1 John 3:1-8
John 10:11-18	John 10:11-18	John 10:11-16	John 10:11-18	John 10:11-18

EXEGESIS

First Lesson: Acts 4:23-37. After the healing of the man lame from birth and the arrest and interrogation of Peter and John, Acts depicts their release and return to the Christian community. This peaceful resolution of the incident affords Luke the opportunity to continue his idealized picture of the primitive church of Jerusalem at prayer and enjoying a common life of sharing resources. One might have expected a prayer of thanksgiving for the release of the apostles; instead the prayer petitions God for strength and support in the preaching mission of the church. The prayer is a plausible one, in Jewish or OT style (see Isa. 37:16-20 for a model), but it contains in vv. 27-28 a rather strained exegesis of the quotation from Ps. 2:1-2 which reflects the characteristically Lucan theme of promise (the psalm) and fulfillment (the passion of Jesus). The psalm refers to Gentile opposition to Yahweh and his anointed king. The interpretation refers to the combined Gentile and Jewish (note the unusual plural, "the peoples of Israel") persecution of Jesus as the Messiah (the anointed one). The petition for healing and signs and wonders to accompany the apostolic preaching, of course, refers backward to the healing of the lame man and forward to other incidents in Acts.

V. 32 introduces one of the Lucan summary passages, emphasizing the sharing of goods in the community and paving the way for the story of Ananias and Sapphira in the next chapter. It also introduces Barnabas the Cypriot, who will play a major role in the early period of Paul's missionary activity.

Second Lesson: 1 John 3:1-8. These verses are part of a longer unit of thought that begins with the last two verses of chap. 2, and it would be advisable to read the latter to understand the passage better. The whole passage reminds us of the difficulty in this Epistle of knowing whether third-person pronouns refer to God or to Christ. Despite the fact that the name Jesus and the title Christ do not appear in these verses, there is little doubt that from v. 2b on the reference is to Christ. The tendency of the author toward such an apparent ambiguity may not be entirely accidental, for he carries forward the Johannine theme of the close relationship between the Father and the Son: "He who confesses the Son has the Father also" (2:23). Closely connected with this theme in the Fourth Gospel is that of being children of God (see John 1:12), which for the Epistle is synonymous with being a believer in Jesus. In both writings being a child of God is God's own gift, the product of his love (3:1; John 1:12), but while in the Gospel the gift is contingent upon believing in Jesus, in the Epistle it is also contingent upon righteous behavior (2:29; 3:10), of which love of one another is the principal manifestation.

Unlike the Fourth Gospel, the Epistle is clearly oriented toward a future eschatology of which the pivotal point is the Second Coming of

The Fourth Sunday of Easter

Christ. This is explicitly mentioned in 2:28 and repeated in 3:2. Despite a tradition of interpretation reaching far back into antiquity, it is possible to understand this famous verse rather differently: "Beloved, we are God's children now, and he has not yet appeared. What we shall be we know because when he appears, we shall be like him, for we shall see him as he is." Though it improves the logic of the verse, this translation wins little support among commentators. In any case, what is important for the author is the fact that hope in the Second Coming determines the believer's attitude in the present. The opposite of righteous behavior is sin, and these two modes of existence divide people with a sharpness that is reminiscent of the Fourth Gospel. There, in the heat of polemic against "the Jews," it is Jesus who charges them with being of their "father the devil" (John 8:44); this is also a context in which sin (in the limited sense of the Fourth Gospel) is at issue (8:34). In the Epistle we are dealing with polemic against those who have deserted the community, who claim not to have sinned (1:8–10) but in reality are sinners by virtue of the fact that they have broken the bond of association with Jesus (v. 6).

Gospel: John 10:11–18. It is important to situate these verses in the larger context of the discourse in chap. 10. The discourse begins (vv. 1–5) with the closest Johannine parallel to the parables of Jesus which are characteristic of the Synoptic tradition. Underlying these initial verses are several parables about shepherd and sheep. The evangelist interprets these parables allegorically with separate explanations, identifying Jesus with the door of the sheep and, in our pericope, with the good shepherd. The use of sheep and shepherd imagery in antiquity is very widespread, both in Hellenistic religious literature and in the OT and NT. The Fourth Gospel may be reinterpreting sayings of Jesus such as we find in Luke 15:4–7 and Matt. 18:12–14 (the parable of the lost sheep), or it may be dependent on the OT tradition in which Yahweh is called a shepherd (Psalm 23) and the leaders of Israel, good and bad, are compared to shepherds (e.g., Ezek. 34:1–31). Typical of the christocentric character of the Fourth Gospel, it is Jesus who is the "good" (the model or ideal) shepherd, identified in a characteristic Johannine "I am" saying.

The Johannine reinterpretation of traditions, however, goes far beyond the traditions themselves in several respects which are not part of the OT imagery. First there is the theme of mutual knowing of the shepherd and the sheep expressed in v. 14, commenting on vv. 3–5. Such knowing and being known is central to the Johannine theology and rooted in the mutual knowing and love of the Father and the Son.

Second, and more prominently in the passage there is the theme of the shepherd laying down his life for the sheep. This is much more than the notion that a good shepherd risks his life for his flock, a notion that is not unknown to the traditional imagery. Instead it is an interpretation of the saving death of Jesus for his friends (cf. 15:13). V. 18 emphasizes Jesus' autonomy in his passion and death, as is characteristic of the Johannine passion narrative, but this lofty christological statement is tempered by the idea that Jesus' "power" is a charge or command of the Father.

Finally, perhaps the most distinctive element of this commentary on the parable of vv. 1–5 is the reference to "other sheep" and the "one flock" in v. 16. Though it is clearly an interpretation of the parable, as the language shows, this verse interrupts the continuity of its immediate context and may be an interpolation made at a late stage in the complex development of the Gospel. Traditionally it is regarded as an allusion to the Gentile mission of the church, but more recently it has been taken as a reference to other, non-Johannine Christian communities with which the Johannine church desires unity. The "sheep," after all, are probably already Christians. In any case, v. 16 is an eloquent appeal to Christian unity and universality.

HOMILETICAL INTERPRETATION

The three appointed readings present us with three aspects of the life of the church in the world whose relationship can best be seen when they are treated backward: Gospel, Second Lesson, First Lesson. (The great Lutheran preacher of the last generation Paul Scherer used to tell his students that it was often illuminating to deal with biblical texts backward.) In this case, the Gospel presents us with the dependence of the church on the atoning life and death of Jesus (see the exegesis). The Epistle then talks about what it means to be an *individual* disciple who "abides in him" (see the exegesis). The reading from Acts describes the life of a *fellowship* of believers, in terms of their inner unity and the outward manifestations of the power of the Spirit.

One also notices in all the readings the pervasive presence of a hostile environment—the world. "The kings of the earth set themselves in array and the rulers were gathered together against the Lord and against his Anointed" (Acts 4:26). "He who does right is righteous . . . he who commits sin is of the devil" (1 John 3:8). The hireling and the shepherd in the Gospel pericope represent the antithesis. One of the things which might be addressed on this Sunday is the hostility the church encounters in the world. In many lands it is a basic fact of life, and it seems to

The Fourth Sunday of Easter

increase with the commitment of Christians to the Lord. It may be helpful to point out this feature of life in the church to congregations who are not used to hostility and might be surprised or even offended by it. This theme recurs in later weeks of the Easter season.

First Lesson: Acts 4:23-37. This lesson is appropriate for the Easter season because of its basic thrust. The church as a community of believers is filled with the Holy Spirit. It speaks the word of God with boldness. God heals and performs signs and wonders through its members, who act "through the name of thy holy Servant Jesus." Such healing and wonders are prayed for in this lesson, although in the lesson from Acts read the Third Sunday of Easter a healing was already referred to and two weeks ago one was actually described. Christians held property in common, and there was no need among them.

We may agree with the exegesis that such a description of life in the church is idealized. Most of us do not have such absolute devotion (nor, we should add, such a sense of the impending end of the world) as the earliest disciples. Yet modern disciples should learn to confront every item in this description of life in the first Christian community as pointing the direction for the growth of the church. If we cannot claim them for ourselves, why not?

Do we pray for the presence of the Spirit? Are we prepared to encounter the awesome power of the Spirit's presence? Or do we simply shrug and say that the Spirit came once long ago?

Are we prepared to "speak thy word with all boldness"? There are, of course, many ways to speak the word. We are not all called to be preachers, and people who are all the time talking about religion and faith often alienate hearers. But is it not more of a danger that when the time comes we will not have any word to say about the greatness and wonders and mercy of God?

Do we expect great things to happen? If we expect nothing, it is more than likely that nothing will happen.

Do we share what possessions we have? Love has a way of unlocking the viselike grip with which many of us hold onto our property. Generous giving is not a precondition for receiving God's grace, but it is a sign that grace has been received! Recall John Wesley's advice: "Earn all you can, save all you can, give all you can."

Second Lesson: 1 John 3:1-8. Here our attention is directed not to the life of the Christian community but to the lives of the individuals who comprise it. The presence of both individual and corporate emphasis reminds us that when we live in the Spirit which comes from Christ both these elements are present, and present equally. The Christian group is not a totalitarian society of nameless faces nor is it a casual assembly of Spirit-filled individuals. It is a society of love to which individuals contribute their peculiar gifts and from which they draw the right and the freedom to be themselves.

The crucial phrase in this pericope is "abiding in him." "No one who abides in him sins" (v. 6). To be filled with the Spirit is to abide in Christ. We are to be like him, for we are all children of God: he by "nature" from the beginning, we by "adoption and grace." (Cf. John 1:12 and the ancient collect for Christmas Day.) We are children of God "in him," for we abide in him in the Spirit.

To be "in him," this lesson tells us, has certain consequences of a moral nature (see the exegesis). We do not sin, for example. The power of the Spirit, working in us and through us, not only teaches us the things that are right, but in the words of another ancient collect gives us "grace and power faithfully to accomplish them."

Perhaps even more important is the recognition that "in the world" we are not likely to be prefect and that to be "in him" means a process of purification. Even when we fail, we are not cut off from the presence or mercy of God. To be "in him" is to be kept close to God in a relationship of continual illumination and correction.

Perhaps even more important than being righteous or being in the process of becoming righteous is "being *like* him" (v. 2). We are God's children *now*. We may not know exactly what it means to be righteous in any given situation. "New occasions teach new duties." But to be "in him" provides us with a Spirit which can discern what new duties are, and thereby the possibility of being faithful amid the most confusing and perplexing circumstances.

Gospel: John 10:11–18. As the exegesis informs us, the image of the Good Shepherd and the sheep is as close as the Fourth Gospel comes to a synoptic parable. The language of shepherd and sheep appears frequently, both in the other Gospels and in the OT, to describe Israel's relation to God or God's Messiah.

Three motifs are particularly suggestive for homiletic development. First is the shepherd who "lays down his life for his sheep." As the exegesis states, this is a Fourth Gospel reference to the atoning death of Jesus. That death distinguishes the Good Shepherd from the hireling and establishes the depth of the love which characterizes both the indwelling of Father and Son and the indwelling of Son and disciples. "I am the good shepherd; I know my own and my own know me, as the Father knows me and I know the Father; and I lay down my life for the sheep"

(vv. 14–15). The word "know" is to be understood in this context as implying the fullness of personal relationship involved in the Hebrew *yādah*. The preacher is invited to explore how people who love each other deeply know each other instinctively.

The second interesting motif in this passage is that of the "other sheep that are not of this fold" (v. 16). Whether this refers to those who do not yet believe in Jesus as the Christ or, as the exegesis suggests, to Christians of another persuasion, our eyes are unquestionably lifted to see the universality of the Good Shepherd's love and of the Father's love communicated by the Good Shepherd. It is precisely *because* Christians are committed to God's revelation of himself through Jesus that they are able to recognize other revelations of God in other times and places. Among believers in other faiths, as among us, there are those who will hear the voice of the Good Shepherd and follow him as the fulfillment of all truth.

The third significant motif is that of the hireling who cares nothing for the sheep. We live in a world teeming with religious leaders all of whom claim to be bearers of the truth. The criterion for recognition of the Good Shepherd in this situation is at once simple and devastating. The Good Shepherd dies for his sheep; he gives himself for them, that they may live. The James Joneses of Jonestown and the Khomeinis of this world are weighed in the balance of that scale and found wanting.

The Fifth Sunday of Easter

Lutheran	Roman Catholic	Episcopal	Pres/UCC/Chr	Meth/COCU
Acts 8:26–40	Acts 9:26–31	Acts 8:26–40 or Deut. 4:32–40	Acts 9:26–31	Acts 8:26–40 or Acts 9:26–31 or Deut. 4:32–40
1 John 3:18–24	1 John 3:18–24	1 John 3:(14–17) 18–24 or Acts 8:26–40	1 John 3:18–24	1 John 3:18–24
John 15:1–8	John 15:1–8	John 14:15–21	John 15:1–8	John 15:1–8

EXEGESIS

First Lesson: Acts 8:26–40. This charming story of the missionary activity of Philip, one of the seven whose appointment is described in

Acts 6:1-6, illustrates further the mission of the Hellenistic Jewish Christians beyond Jerusalem (cf. 8:1). Given the solemnity with which Luke invests Peter's conversion of the Gentile Cornelius in chap. 10, this incident should probably not be regarded as the first overture to the Gentiles. The Ethiopian official, who worships in Jerusalem and reads Isaiah, is portrayed as a Jew or at least a proselyte to Judaism. As is typical of many important events in the Book of Acts, it is, of course, God who orchestrates the spread of the Christian mission: an angel of the Lord initiates Philip's journey and the Spirit guides his actions on the way.

The Ethiopian is reading Isa. 53:7-8, a part of the famous suffering servant passage which undoubtedly played a significant role in the development of early Christian reflection on the person and role of Christ. The passage is not often quoted explicitly in the NT, however, and the place of suffering servant Christology is sometimes exaggerated in modern assessments of the earliest christological development. The passage is more important as an illustration of the role played by the Christian reinterpretation of the OT in the development of Christian theology. For the early Christians, only the Christian community could guide one in understanding the Scriptures.

Most modern versions of the Bible omit v. 37: "And Philip said, 'If you believe with all your heart, you may.' And he replied, 'I believe that Jesus Christ is the Son of God.'" This verse is not well represented in the ancient manuscripts, and it undoubtedly reflects the developing baptismal discipline of the later church.

Second Lesson: 1 John 3:18-24. This passage is actually the conclusion of the same sense unit to which the corresponding reading of the previous Sunday belongs. Between the two passages lie some very concrete instructions on the love of one another, which v. 18, reminiscent of the very practical exhortations of the Epistle of James, summarizes. In fact, if we had only the Gospel of John, we would have very little idea of how love in the Johannine community was practiced. The First Epistle attempts, modestly to be sure, to remedy the possible vagueness of the Gospel's message. Love "in deed and in truth"—sharing the world's goods with the brother who is in need (v. 17)—provides the reassurance that one can stand before God with a heart (or conscience) that does not accuse but inspires confidence.

This passage illustrates a familiar trait of Johannine language, the interchange of singular and plural in such words as "sin" and "commandment." Although he is interested in righteous behavior, the author of the Epistle does not allude here to the commandments of the Decalogue; rather, in v. 23, he spells out precisely what God commands. In the Farewell Discourses in the Gospel Jesus commanded us to love one another. The Epistle sums up the Gospel message more broadly by including belief in the name of Jesus Christ as part of God's commandment. In the polemical context of schism in the Johannine church, both correct faith and loving behavior are important.

The pericope concludes with a very significant statement about "abiding," but since the third-person pronouns in v. 24 are in all likelihood references to God rather than to Christ, here it is said that believers abide in God and God in them, without the mediatorial role of Christ being explicitly mentioned. It is implicitly present, however, because the mutual indwelling is contingent upon both love and faith in Jesus Christ. Moreover, in the Farewell Discourses Jesus had promised that he, or God, would send the Spirit after his return to the Father. Now the presence of the Spirit is the evidence that God abides in the believers. Since the Spirit is God's gift, we are reminded that both faith and love, made possible by the Spirit, are also God's gracious gifts to the Christian community.

Gospel: John 15:1-8. This passage is in some ways quite similar to the pericope from John 10 read the preceding Sunday. It is in part an allegorical interpretation of what may be traditional parabolic material, but in this case the interpretation begins abruptly and the parable or other saying is not quoted. Some have guessed that underlying this Johannine discourse is some form of the saying of Jesus, connected with the Last Supper, found in Mark 14:25 and parallels "I shall not drink again of the fruit of the vine until that day when I drink it new in the kingdom of God." However inviting, this must remain only a conjecture, for like the imagery of shepherd and sheep, that of the vine or the vineyard is very widespread in the OT (e.g., Isa. 5:1-7 or Ps. 80:8-16) in some of the parables of Jesus, and in other contemporary literature. John's choice of symbols is often dictated by their universality rather than by a specific allusion.

There are two venerable traditions of interpretation of our pericope which should probably be ruled out in advance: the eucharistic and the ecclesiological. Perhaps because the Farewell Discourses are set in the context of the Johannine Last Supper, or perhaps because of their supposed connection with Mark 14:25, numerous interpreters have tried to see in these verses an allusion to the eucharistic wine functioning as a counterpart to the bread of chap. 6. It should be observed, however, that there is no mention of wine in John 15 and, indeed, no clear allusion to the Eucharist anywhere in John 13—17. Any eucharistic interpretation of the passage would rest on very tenuous grounds. Similarly, it is unlikely that the vine imagery is intended to symbolize the church, for there is no emphasis on the vine with its branches as a collective image. Instead, the interpretation has to do with the disciples' (the believers') intimate relationship with Christ as the source of their power to "bear fruit." Typically, the Fourth Gospel treats believers as individuals, but its thought should not therefore be called individualistic. The emphasis on love for one another counteracts any real individualism.

Though the disciples are not formally identified with the branches until v. 5, there is an implicit identification in v. 3 which depends on a play on words that modern translations do not always reflect. The word translated as "prunes" in v. 2 is cognate to the word for "clean" in v. 3 and bears both meanings. In the agricultural metaphor the disciples have already been "pruned" by the revealing word of Jesus; at the same time they have been purified in a religious sense.

It is not immediately apparent what "bearing fruit" means, and it may be that the lectionary has cut off the passage a few verses too early. It becomes clear, as the following Sunday's Gospel shows, that the supreme manifestation of bearing fruit is the love of Christ and the love of one another.

HOMILETICAL INTERPRETATION

One theme which unites the three lessons appointed for this Sunday is membership. The First Lesson describes baptism, the act by which one joins the community of faith in Jesus Christ. The Second Lesson and the Gospel are at one in speaking of the members of the community, the "branches," as abiding in Christ (cf. 1 John 3:24; John 15:4; and passim).

A sermon on this theme as it comes before us in these three lessons would have to undertake at least two difficult but rewarding tasks. The first would be to wrestle with the mystery of the priority of God's grace to any human response of either belief or obedience.

In the reading from Acts it might seem at first inspection that the Ethiopian eunuch took the initiative in seeking baptism and professing faith. Yet on closer pondering, one sees how the way was prepared for that initiative through Philip's presence, by the leading of an "angel" (v. 26), or under the guidance of the Spirit (v. 39). (We might venture to think that the angel and the Spirit are equivalent expressions here.) We also notice that the Ethiopian had been reading an OT passage, which Philip was providentially at hand to interpret (see the exegesis).

Similarly, in the Second Lesson we are told to "believe in the name of his Son Jesus Christ and to love one another" (v. 23). Yet "we know that he abides in us by the Spirit which he has given us," making both faith and love possible. Is the initiative ours or his?

In the Gospel, disciples are bidden to bear much fruit, yet "as the branch cannot bear fruit by itself, unless it abides in the vine, neither can you unless you abide in me." Ultimately the initiative is God's. As a familiar hymn runs:

> I find, I walk, I love, but O the whole
> Of love is but my answer, Lord, to thee;
> For thou wert love beforehand with my soul,
> Always thou lovest me.
> *The Hymnal 1940* No. 405

The second task of the sermon would be to deal with the equal importance of faith and love, of word and deed. If in baptism the emphasis falls on faith, the life of the community subsequently depends on love expressed "in deed and truth" (1 John 3:18).

First Lesson: Acts 8:26-40. Philip's encounter with the Ethiopian minister is an early instance of the spread of the Christian message beyond the limits of Judea.

One might regard this lesson from the viewpoint of the church, as a time when a church member was "filled with the Holy Spirit and spoke the word of God with boldness" (in the words of last week's reading from Acts 4:31). The rich inner life of the church fed by the Spirit of Christ leads to missionary outreach. If the preacher is at work on a series of sermons on the life of the church in the Spirit, here we see the church moving into the world.

One might be tempted to speak of the mission of the church as a "response" to what God has done in Christ, but such an expression would not be precise, for it might suggest that missionary activity is a kind of obligation unwillingly accepted. This is often the case in contemporary Christianity. It is closer to this lesson, however, and to the NT to regard the mission of the church as the work of the Spirit flowing over and beyond the limits set by existing boundaries. Throughout this passage Philip operates under the power of the Spirit, as the Spirit's agent, with freedom and joy.

The fact that the Ethiopian was reading the scroll of Isaiah points to the fact that the way of the gospel is well prepared ahead of time, for God has never left himself without witnesses. The scroll provoked a question which Philip answered with "the good news of Jesus" (v. 35). The preacher might ask himself or herself and the congregation to try to identify God at work in the world beyond the church either through the quest for justice and truth, which the church can affirm, or through the raising of questions about the meaning of life, to which the gospel can be seen as a resolution. The way of the gospel is still prepared ahead of time.

One could also regard this lesson as an illustration of baptism. The crucial elements are all at hand: the proclamation of the good news of Jesus, the awakening of faith in the candidate, his taking the initiative (at least apparently) to seek baptism, and (reading the omitted verse, especially if, as the exegesis suggests, it is indicative of the practice of some early community) the profession of faith in Jesus Christ as the Son of God. A sermon on this subject, even if no baptism is performed, can put the congregation in mind of their own baptism—the importance of the life-giving word which evokes faith—and the significance of the commitment which baptism implies.

Second Lesson: 1 John 3:18–24. We might note here the stress on confidence in God, and consequently confidence and boldness in life. In this age of widespread insecurity and anxiety, it is an absolutely essential dimension of the gospel.

We have already seen that on the one hand "we receive from him whatever we ask because we keep his commandments" (v. 22) and on the other hand, we keep his commandments to believe in Jesus Christ and to love one another "by the Spirit which he has given us" (v. 24). By that Spirit he abides in us and we in him.

We might also recall that in last week's reading from 1 John there is a clear ethical dimension to "abiding in him." "No one who abides in him sins" (3:6). The life of the Spirit is a life of abiding in Christ, in which sin is impossible, faith abundant, love overflowing, and confidence the inevitable outcome.

Gospel: John 15:1–8. This week, the Gospel reinforces most of the themes enunciated in the Epistle, under the familiar image of branches and vine.

The image permits an important insight into the nature of "abiding." The relation between vine and branches is subtly different from the relation between head and members (1 Cor. 12:12ff.) to which it is often compared. For both head and members are parts that together comprise a whole. But the vine is the whole, including the branches. The branches, though they are parts of the vine, do not make up the vine by a process of addition. The branches do not have life in themselves—the life belongs to the vine!

Through the figure of pruning, the image also affords the introduction of the idea of purification and judgment into the "abiding." Branches which do not "bear fruit" are cut off. Bearing fruit is to "keep my commandment that you love one another" (vv. 10 and 12). Branches which do not bear fruit do not manifest the life of the vine; hence they do not belong in the vine. Yet even the branches which do bear fruit are pruned to bear more fruit. A sermon on this text can raise the sensitive question of evil and how Christians can respond to it. If they abide in the vine, evil or judgment will seem like the pruning of purification, painful but not ultimately destructive. If one does not abide in the vine and has none of the life of the Spirit, evil will prove to be destructive.

One must be careful to avoid implying any kind of merit theology. One bears fruit by virtue of the life in the vine, not by virtue of the effort of the branch. One keeps the commandments and does them by the power of the Spirit in which the church abides.

The Sixth Sunday of Easter

Lutheran	Roman Catholic	Episcopal	Pres/UCC/Chr	Meth/COCU
Acts 11:19–30	Acts 10:25–26, 34–35, 44–48	Acts 11:19–30 or Isa. 45:11–13, 18–19	Acts 10:34–48	Acts 11:19–30 or Isa. 45:11–13, 18–19
1 John 4:1–11	1 John 4:7–10	1 John 4:7–21 or Acts 11:19–30	1 John 4:1–7	1 John 4:1–11
John 15:9–17	John 15:9–17	John 15:9–17	John 15:9–17	John 15:9–17

EXEGESIS

First Lesson: Acts 11:19–30. This section of the Book of Acts gives rise to several complex historical questions which it is not possible to discuss here. Instead it will be useful, and a prior exegetical task in any case, to observe some of Luke's literary intentions in making use of traditions about the important early Christian community in the Syrian city of Antioch. After telling in elaborate detail of the conversion of the Gentile Cornelius, Luke can now turn to a brief account of the establishing of the first predominantly Gentile church. It is the work of the Hellenist, or Greek-speaking Jewish Christians from Jerusalem, but Luke is at pains to show that Paul (still called Saul, who is to be the founder par excellence of Gentile churches) was associated with the Antioch church early in its history. The word translated as "Greeks" in v. 20 presents a notorious textual problem. The more likely reading is "Hellenists," but that term cannot have its usual meaning here, for the contrast with "Jews" in v. 19 demands that it refer to Gentiles.

The statement that "in Antioch the disciples were for the first time called Christians" is somewhat puzzling, for the Greek word seems in form to be of Latin origin. The word is rare in early Christian literature, occuring elsewhere in the NT only in Acts 26:28 (on the lips of King Agrippa) and in 1 Pet. 4:16. It is quite possible that the term was coined by Gentile opponents of the Christian or by Roman officials and only later won proud acceptance by the Christians themselves. The favorite term for Christians in Acts, as our passage shows, is "disciples."

Second Lesson: 1 John 4:1-11. Like the preceding passage, which was last read Sunday, this reading typically juxtaposes the two themes of correct faith and love for one another. But here the context is more explicitly polemical, we learn more about what was at issue from a doctrinal viewpoint between the Johannine community and those who seceded from it. The latter are condemned in strong terms as false prophets and as an embodiment of the "antichrist"—an eschatological opponent of the Messiah in the author's view (v. 3). The doctrinal issue is their refusal to make a public confession of faith—probably in liturgical settings—in the true humanity of the Son of God: "that Jesus Christ has come in the flesh" (v. 2). Though details are scarce, we may suppose that they were tending toward a radically otherworldly understanding of Jesus as a purely spiritual divine emissary, something like what we find in Gnostic writings. Despite his own tendency toward dualism, the author insists that the Son whom the Father sent as Savior of the world (v. 14) was the human Jesus. For John the issue is the test of whether the spirit that animates the Christian is really God's Spirit or a spirit opposed to God, a spirit of truth or a spirit of error.

The second part of the reading (vv. 7-11) returns, as frequently in the Epistle, to the theme of love for one another. But this time the motivation for such love is different. Love is not merely the fulfillment of a commandment (of Christ or of God), but practicing love is a way of knowing God, "for God is love." This lofty statement climaxes the theological viewpoint of the Epistle and relates it to the lives of the believers. God's love is in his gracious initiative in the process of saving humanity through his Son. Loving one another is the supreme human response to that initiative.

The Sixth Sunday of Easter

Gospel: John 15:9–17. The Gospel reading is also the immediate sequel to that of the previous Sunday, and it spells out more clearly than before what it means for the branches of the vine to bear fruit. The reading begins somewhat abruptly by defining the concept of mutual "abiding," introduced in vv. 4–5, as a relationship of love. It goes further, however, by linking the Father's love for Jesus, Jesus' love for his disciples, and the disciples' love for one another (the "commandments") in a chain of interdependent relationships. The role of Jesus as mediator of the divine love is much more clearly emphasized in the Gospel than in the Epistle, illustrating the christocentric character of the Gospel over against the more theocentric character of the Epistle.

Jesus' commandment to love one another plays a central role in the Farewell Discourses. When first introduced, in John 13:34, it is described as a "new" commandment. Since love of neighbor was a not uncommon injunction even in the OT (e.g., Lev. 19:18), one needs to ask what is new about Jesus' commandment. The answer most likely lies in the qualification "as I have loved you," which appears both in John 13:34 and here in 15:12. It is in the past tense because the perspective of the Farewell Discourses is a post-Easter one. The actual extent of Jesus' love for his friends is eloquently spelled out in v. 13 in proverbial style but with an unmistakable application to the death of Jesus (cf. John 10:11–18). Jesus' death is that of the shepherd laying down his life for his sheep, the friend laying down his life for his friends. In the overall context of the Fourth Gospel it is the ultimate revelation of God's love.

V. 16 is another form of the typically Johannine idea that the initiative toward salvation does not come from the saved but from God. Given the christocentrism of the Gospel, it is Jesus who has chosen his followers and empowered them (vv. 5–7) to bear fruit and receive whatever they request from the Father. The larger context suggests that what they should be asking for is the ability to love one another, though the notion of other prayerful requests is not excluded.

HOMILETICAL INTERPRETATION

The teaching which underlies all three lessons appointed for the Sixth Sunday of Easter is that Christians are to love each other as Christ has loved them. Each lesson makes its own contribution to the archetypal Christian theme, and a three-point sermon might well be constructed around the three lessons, beginning with the Gospel. As the exegesis shows, the new thing which Jesus adds to the commandment to love one's neighbors is the concluding phrase "as I have loved you." It is a love which knows no limits. It is a love which is willing to surrender life itself for the other. The love which unites Christian disciples is the love which Jesus exemplified and which is accessible to believers by "abiding in him" through the Spirit. The love at the heart of the Christian proclamation is the limitless love of God with which he loves the Son and with which the Son loves those whom he chooses.

The reading from 1 John underlines all these points: "In this is love, not that we loved God but that he loved us and sent his Son to be the expiation for our sins" (v. 10). The note of atonement here is more explicit, but the distinctive note is the criterion for testing the spirits. In a time when charismatic movements have made the church particularly aware of the life of the Spirit, it is pertinent to note that from NT times on, it has been recognized that human beings live in a welter of spirits. The choice people face is not so much between Holy Spirit and *no* spirit but between Holy Spirit and false spirits, some of which are both powerful and deceptive: the spirit of nationalism, for example, or the spirit of alternative religions. How does one know the true spirit? The test proposed in our lesson is a clear one: "Every spirit which confesses that Jesus Christ has come in the flesh is of God, and every spirit which does not confess Jesus is not of God." (Cf. Paul's criterion, proposed under somewhat similar circumstances: "No one can say that 'Jesus is Lord,' except by the Holy Spirit" [1 Cor. 12:31].)

The first reading from Acts represents what we might call an external, as opposed to an internal, description of life in the Spirit. In Antioch, Christians proclaimed Jesus Christ as Lord to all comers, not to Jews only. Love shows itself limitless not only in depth and inwardly but also in extent and outwardly. What is more, the extension of the church's mission was greeted with approval by Barnabas, the representative of the central Jerusalem establishment. The new community was nourished in faith by the teaching of Paul, and when famine reduced the Jerusalem church to need, the new Antiochene Christians demonstrated their love for their neighbors concretely, by sending relief to the Jerusalem church through Barnabas and Paul. It was the first recorded instance, but surely not the last, of mission in reverse. The discovery that sending churches need the ministration of younger churches has been made anew in our day, to our endless profit.

The title of a sermon based on all three lessons thus might be "The New Commandment," and its points could be: the priority of God's love for us in Christ; the test of the new Spirit as the confession of Jesus; and the life of the new Spirit as the welcoming of the new and the preservation of the old.

The Sixth Sunday of Easter

First Lesson: Acts 11:19-30. We have already called attention to a number of the features of this passage which might commend it to the preacher. In particular, if one has decided to preach a series of sermons on the life of the church in the world, this text, following on the missionary activity and baptism in last week's reading from Acts, shows the way in which a new unit of the church is nurtured and sustained.

The openness and welcome of the Jerusalem church stands as a clear signal against the instinct of many Christian groups to discourage newcomers. We read that when Barnabas came down from Jerusalem "he saw the grace of God and he was glad" (v. 23). Are we glad when we see the grace of God operating powerfully in other people, newcomers to Christ? Isn't it easy to suppose that new zeal is excessive and needs to be dampened instead of encouraged? Don't we sometimes feel jealous or suspicious of new movements and new voices in the church?

The passage also raises the question of church growth, as do many references in the Book of Acts. "A large company was added to the Lord" (v. 24b; cf. 2:41; 4:4; 6:1, 7; 13:43; etc.). Crowds regularly gathered about Jesus too, and everyone heard him gladly. One would expect that a word which brings peace in place of anxiety, forgiveness for guilt, and life from death would attract many. There are no limits on the gospel message. It is intended for all persons, in all times and in all places. On the other hand, there is an alienating and affronting character to it. It unmasks all hypocrisy and pretense, and the powers of this world resent it, as this century has seen in Germany, Russia, and many other parts of the world (and also in the eighteenth century in France). A whole sermon might be built around the tension between the popularity of the gospel and the danger of selling out to the world, or between the unpopularity of the gospel and the danger of establishing an exclusive and elitist group. Such an approach would invite a resolution from the criterion set forward in the Second Lesson for "testing the spirits."

Barnabas also provided for the instruction of the new community by bringing Saul (Paul) from Tarsus. Surely none better! Paul taught for a whole year, and we might venture to think that a congregation which began with a teaching mission like that never ceased to learn the inexhaustible truth of the gospel. After proclamation, teaching; after conversion, nurture—that is a perennial rhythm in Christian life.

Enough has been said about the significance of the "reverse mission." Congregations are responsible for each other in the Lord. The Book of Acts reminds us that "it is more blessed to give than to receive" (20:35). We trust that the offering was gracefully received in Jerusalem and that in our time we may gracefully receive the ministration of churches younger in the faith than ourselves. We are all "partners in mission."

Second Lesson: 1 John 4:1-11. Martin Luther called the eighth chapter of Romans "the clearest gospel of them all." The same judgment might be made about the fourth chapter of 1 John. It contains the lapidary formula which for many is the summary of God's revelation in Christ: "God is love." It maintains the divine initiative ("not that we loved God . . .") and it puts the relation between God's love for us and our love for our neighbors in the typical Johannine way which allows us to see the latter as the fruit of the former. No danger of works-righteousness here!

The chapter does contain, however, an incipient dualism: "They are of the world. . . . We are of God" (vv. 5-6). A preacher might do worse than devote a sermon to the Christian's attitude toward the world, which this passage suggests and which so much in the Christian tradition reinforces. The old baptismal service, for example contained a renunciation of "the world, the flesh, and the devil." On the other hand, God made the world and saw that it was very good. Human beings, in the image of God, stand at the apex of that creation. It might be helpful to explore that tension with the information that in the Johannine literature and in the works of other Christian authors "world" is understood to mean not the world as created by God but the world as distorted by sin—the world "with God included out," to use an expression of Sam Goldwyn's. Between the disciple and the world in the latter sense there must be opposition and hostility, and the description in this passage of the world and the spirit of error is just. Yet Christ died to redeem the world in the former sense. In Christian life, dualism is temporary and at most penultimate. In the end God will be "all in all" (1 Cor. 15:28).

Gospel: John 15:9-17. We have already spoken above and in the homiletical interpretation of the lessons for the Fifth Sunday of Easter, about "loving one another as I have loved you." Two points deserve closer attention, and perhaps either could be developed into a sermon.

One is the emphasis on friendship. "You are my friends if you do what I command you. No longer do I call you servants, but friends" (vv. 13-15). So much is made of servanthood in the NT that one should hesitate to call it into question on the basis of this one passage, especially in view of the paradoxical "You are my friends if you do what I command you." The way to resolve the tension which is set up here lies in the nature of "abiding." To abide in Christ, or in his love, makes us able to love with his love. Therefore one obeys the commandment to love, not grudgingly or with prospect of reward in view—obedience represents what one is freed to do and does freely. Therefore any overtones of unwillingness or subservience which might be carried by the term "servant" are banished. Friendship is the beautiful relation which results. Surely there is a sermon in the phrase "friends of God."

Second is the doctrine of election implied in the verse, "You did not choose me, but I chose you" (v. 16). Almost no doctrine is less understood and more suspect among modern Christians than this. Its appearance in this passage allows us to see the relation between election and love. Imagine the conversation: "Dearest, I love you." "Why, what can you find in me to love?" "I love you because I love everyone." The human lover in this instance deserves a slap in the face. Love is never general, but always particular. It always requires choice or election. Even if we were to transfer that hypothetical conversation to the relation between God and humanity, we might come to the same conclusion. God loves each person separately for himself or herself, by choice, by election. We might believe (as I do) that God loves all humankind. But he does not love us in general. There is no universal proposition from which I deduce that God loves me. I discover that God loves me for myself, by election and grace. That is the wonder of the gospel. Love as a universal principle is not good news. Election is.

The Ascension of Our Lord

Lutheran	Roman Catholic	Episcopal	Pres/UCC/Chr	Meth/COCU
Acts 1:1–11	Acts 1:1–11	Acts 1:1–11 or Ezek. 1:3–5a, 15–22, 26–28	Acts 1:1–11	Acts 1:1–11 or Ezek. 1:3–5a, 15–22, 26–28
Eph. 1:16–23	Eph. 1:17–23	Eph. 1:15–23 or Acts 1:1–11	Eph. 1:16–23	Eph. 1:15–23
Luke 24:44–53	Mark 16:15–20	Luke 24:49–53 or Mark 16:9–15, 19–20	Luke 28:44–53	Mark 16:9–20 or Luke 24:44–53

EXEGESIS

First Lesson: Ezek. 1:3–5a, 15–22, 26–28. The reading is a composite of verses from the famous throne-chariot vision of Ezekiel. It includes the principal elements of the vision while omitting some of the detailed descriptions. The passage as a whole, like the entire Book of Ezekiel, is a composite, the product of successive reinterpretations of the prophetic and priestly traditions. It is likely that the vision account itself is indebted to the somewhat similar one in Isaiah 6. As the book now stands, the vision of God on his throne-chariot forms the setting for the call of the prophet and indeed highlights the theme of the power and majesty of God which is central to the whole book. It does not seem originally to have been the opening of the book, however, and is not as integral to Ezekiel's prophetic call as the vision of Isaiah was to his.

As always in interpreting visionary literature, one should not press the details too much for consistency or verisimilitude. It is precisely the extravagance of the description that conveys a sense of the awesomeness of God and the powerful impact made on the visionary prophet. The somewhat indistinct character of the vision is emphasized by the frequent use of words such as "likeness" or "appearance" (contrast Isaiah 6). The vision is a theophany and some of the details are the typical signs of a divine appearance: stormy wind, a cloud, brightness, fire, and the like. The "four living creatures" (v. 5), as chap. 10 makes clear, are the cherubim, familiar figures in ancient Near Eastern mythology. The wheels (which become a class of angels in later rabbinic interpretation) symbolize the mobility of the throne-chariot and thus of the presence of God himself. The glory of God, characterized by brightness, is enthroned above the cherubim, as on the ark (cf. Exod. 37:9). This final description is relatively restrained by comparison with that of the cherubim and the wheels.

Second Lesson: Acts 1:1-11. Luke begins the second volume of his work with a somewhat truncated prologue which briefly recalls the prologue to the Gospel. It is followed by a summary of Jesus' postresurrection appearances and instructions to the apostles. Luke had ended his Gospel with an account of the ascension on Easter Sunday itself (Luke 24:50-53). There Jesus was portrayed as imparting a final blessing to his followers and being carried up into heaven (modern interpreters tend to accept the longer text of 24:51). It is surprising, therefore, to find in Acts another and rather different ascension story taking place forty days after Easter. The interpreter's primary task is not to try to reconcile the two stories but to discover the author's particular interests in the Acts narrative. By beginning Acts with what is essentially the last appearance of the risen Lord to the apostles, Luke not only establishes continuity between the Gospel and Acts, but he is able to show that the story of the growth and spread of the church begins with the Lord himself. It is the Holy Spirit whose presence will in fact inaugurate and guide the mission, and the promise of the Spirit is an important part of Jesus' final instructions (vv. 5, 8).

V. 8 is particularly significant in that it places a programmatic statement for the Book of Acts on the lips of Jesus. One expects a literary prologue to a second volume to contain a summary of the contents of the first (vv. 1–5) and an announcement of the contents of the second. Luke has adroitly incorporated the latter into his first narrative. The elements of it are the coming of the Holy Spirit, the role of the apostles as witnesses—a role they share notably with Paul (cf. 22:15; 26:16), who for Luke is not an apostle—and the geographic spread of the church from Jerusalem through Judea to Samaria and beyond. The phrase "to the end of the earth" is derived from Isa. 49:6, which is explicitly quoted by Paul in Acts 13:47. It is generally taken to refer to Rome, the goal of Paul's final journey, and in any case it implies the Gentile mission.

Another important theme in the passage is the eschatological one. Luke uses the story to discourage what is for him no longer an acceptable view, namely, the expectation of a proximate return of Jesus in the full messianic role. This view is what is implied in the apostles' question in v. 6 and in asking it they represent the church in need of eschatological instruction. Jesus' answer in v. 7, based on the saying in Mark 13:32 which Luke has not used in his Gospel, does not negate the importance of the final events of history but only their immediacy. As v. 8 goes on to show, the task of the moment is the missionary one. The same issue is present in the remarks of the interpreting angels after Jesus is taken up (the scene is modeled on the Lucan version of the empty tomb story; cf. Luke 24:4–7). The followers of Jesus are not to "stand looking into heaven" as though in expectation of the Parousia. Nevertheless, though indefinitely future, the Parousia is real, and it is referred to in language which recalls Jesus' own mention of the Son of man "coming in a cloud" (Luke 21:27).

Gospel: Mark 16:9–15, 19–20. The traditional ending of Mark's Gospel, 16:9–20, from which this reading is taken, is certainly not an original part of the Gospel. Besides being completely different in style from the rest of Mark, it is missing in some important ancient manuscripts; others have a different ending. The reading was doubtless chosen because it mentions the ascension (v. 19), but it should not be used as an independent witness to the ascension.

The passage as a whole is composed from incidents in the other Gospels and in Acts of the Apostles or from traditions still being transmitted orally in the second century. The sources are not always clear. For example, v. 12 certainly refers to the appearance to two disciples on the road to Emmaus (Luke 24:13-35), but it is not clear where the appearance to Mary Magdalene (who is described in terms of Luke 8:2) comes from, as there are no echoes of Johannine language. The result of this compositional activity is a short summary of resurrection appearances, the commissioning of the apostles, and the ascension and exaltation of Jesus. The document may well have existed apart from the Gospel of Mark, where it does not fit well in any case. It has its own theological tendency which reflects the concerns of the second-century church. The emphasis is on the absolute necessity of faith in the risen Jesus, on the testimony of eyewitnesses, as the basis for the church's universal mission. The brief mention of the ascension is coupled with a reference to the exaltation of Christ in the language of Ps. 110:1, which was widely used in early Christianity. The signs or miracles mentioned in the last verse are those spelled out in vv. 17-18, which have been omitted from the reading.

HOMILETICAL INTERPRETATION

As suggested in the Foreword, the early church celebrated Pascha from the Day of the Resurrection until Pentecost, during which time the resurrection of Christ, his ascension into heaven, and the coming of the Holy Spirit were celebrated as an undifferentiated whole. They were the Great Fifty Days. As nearly as we can tell, it was not until the fourth century in Jerusalem, during the episcopate of Cyril, that the separate events were singled out for observance on special days and at special places for the benefit of pilgrims to the Holy Land. Pilgrims carried the Jerusalem practice to the ends of the earth so that the commemoration of the ascension of Christ on the fortieth day and the coming of the Spirit on the fiftieth has become virtually universal Christian custom. The time scheme, of course, is that of Luke-Acts. But, as the exegesis points out, even Luke has two accounts of the ascension, one occurring on Easter evening at the end of the Gospel and one on the fortieth day.

It is important to ask a theological question prior to the historical question. What is the function of the ascension of Christ in the Gospel narratives? What does it mean? Perhaps the clearest answer to this question is provided by the Fourth Gospel, which does not record the ascension as an event at all. "I came from the Father and have come into the world; again, I am leaving the world and going to the Father," says Jesus in one of the Farewell Discourses. His disciples replied, "Ah, now you are speaking plainly, not in any figure!" (John 16:28-29).

On this showing, the ascension means the inclusion of Christ into the

Godhead, or more precisely, it represents the belief of the church that the incarnate Son of God was included in the glorious life of the Father. And since the incarnate Son of God had been recognized as Son of man, the representative of the whole human race—at least that is one of the meanings of "Son of man"—ascension means the inclusion of humanity in the life of God.

> Thou hast raised our human nature
>   On the clouds to God's right hand:
> There we sit in heavenly places,
>   There with thee in glory stand.
> Jesus reigns, adored by angels;
> Man with God is on the throne;
> Mighty Lord, in thine ascension,
>   We by faith behold our own.
> *The Hymnal 1940* No. 103

The ascension involves the church in its mission. It announces the commencement of an interim period of unknown duration (Acts 1:7) between the going of the Son of man to the Father and his return in glory (Acts 1:11). This time scheme represents a considerable modification of the original expectation of the church, which anticipated the immediate coming of the Son of man to establish the kingdom of God. But in this interim the Holy Spirit works in the life of believers (Acts 1:8, cf. John 16:7 and Rom. 8:22–23). It is the time of struggle, mission, and hope.

None of the appointed lessons represents a course of readings. All were chosen to illuminate the ascension of the Lord. Ascension is the unifying theme, which the preacher might focus on in a phrase like "Bound for Glory," which would include both Jesus' heavenly destination and that of humanity with him and in him. It might be convenient to reverse the order of the texts: Gospel, lesson from Acts, lesson from Ezekiel.

One account of the ascension is embedded in the last verse of the Gospel according to Mark. As the exegesis indicates, these verses are not originally a part of the Gospel and seem to be a pastiche of incidents from the other Gospels and from Acts. The Lesson was chosen for Cycle B, of course, because this is the year of St. Mark. We read the witness of the Second Gospel to the ascension. The fact that it is included in a brief summary of all the Easter events may be turned to advantage by the preacher, since the liturgical celebration of the season includes the simultaneous celebration of all of them. The ascension is simply one of the motifs of the season. We could speak of "Ascension in the Easter Context."

The reading from Acts, of course, makes the traditional emphasis of the day: Jesus' return to the Father, the expectation of the Spirit, the establishment of an interim time before God's kingdom is established in its fullness, and the call of the church during this time to its mission to be witnesses to Christ to the ends of the earth. We could deal in a second part of the sermon with "Ascension and the Commitment to Mission."

The reading from Ezekiel is a theophany, an expression of the power, the glory, and above all the strangeness of God. It might be taken as a description of the destiny of Jesus, or a way of envisioning what it might be like to be with God. Is there a place for humanity in this awesome splendor? Yes! "Seated above the likeness of a throne was likeness of a *human* form" (Ezek. 1:26). What the prophet saw in a vision afar has become near in the hope of Christians. Ascension celebrates the inclusion of the Son of man into the inner life of God himself. One might dare to speak of "Ascension and the Humanity of God."

First Lesson: Ezek. 1:3-5a; 15-22; 26-28. Aside from what has already been said about this text as a description of "heaven as our destination," we might explore the OT vocabulary which expresses the power, the glory, the omniscience, the omnipresence, the livingness, but above all the otherness of the deity.

The otherness of God is communicated by the cornucopia of bizarre images, by the "great cloud with brightness round about it" (v. 4), and by the repeated use of the term "likeness": "the likeness of a firmament" (v. 22), "the likeness of a throne" (v. 26), "the likeness as it were of a human form" (v. 26). Ordinary human language cannot do justice to the reality of God. Even the most extravagant metaphors cannot adequately express this reality.

The livingness of God is communicated by the livingness of the creatures who surround him, by the extraordinary mobility of the wheels, and especially by the spirit which is in the wheels (v. 21). What is described is not an extraordinary *thing,* but a living being. The mobility of the wheels also suggests the omnipresence of God. Every place is accessible to him; and therefore no place where you and I can go is strange or inaccessible to God. The rims of the wheels "were full of eyes round about" (v. 18), a typically biblical expression for God's all-seeing and all-knowing.

In view of this language which communicates the strangeness and mystery of God, it is particularly noteworthy that we find "the likeness as it were of a human form" seated on the throne. The original of the image in which humanity was created appears at the center of glory. At the conclusion of the chapter note the rainbow, the sign of the covenant of peace between God and his creation (v. 28)! The end of the story—when this destiny is attained—is peace.

Second Lesson: Acts 1:1-11. The remaining obervation to be made about this text is that the assigning of Ascension Day to the fortieth day after Easter rests on this passage alone (v. 8). In view of the fact that Luke himself describes another ascension on Easter evening (Luke 24:50-53), it seems safe to assume that he did not envision a photographable event occurring in a specific chronological relation to Easter. The existential reality surely was that the disciples were vividly aware that the risen Lord was Jesus of Nazareth; but as time went on, they increasingly acknowledged that they had to do with spiritual reality and power, with God himself in a new definition and manifestation—with the Holy Spirit, in short, understood as the Spirit of Jesus Christ.

Gospel: Mark 16:9-15, 19-20. The lapse of time between the resurrection and the ascension is not specified in the Second Gospel. The Second Gospel relates an appearance "in another form to two of them" and "afterward to the Eleven themselves as they sat at table." It would be natural to identify these incidents with parallel ones in Luke, both of which happened on Easter afternoon or evening. In this case, the ascension in Mark, as in Luke, happened on Easter. In Matthew, the ascension occurs in Galilee; consequently a longer period of time must be entailed.

Mark's version of Jesus' parting words, however, is verbally very close to Matthew's and picks up the missionary theme. Although the gift of the Spirit is not mentioned explicitly, it is said that "the Lord worked with them and confirmed the message by the signs that attended it" (v. 20). These signs are enumerated: speaking in tongues, power over "deadly things" (v. 17), and the ability to heal the sick—gifts of the Spirit familiar from Acts and Paul (1 Cor. 12:4-11).

The Easter event involves the empowerment of the church for the duration of history and its equipment for a mission to the world, in the various senses of "world" which we have delineated elsewhere.

The Seventh Sunday of Easter

Lutheran	Roman Catholic	Episcopal	Pres/UCC/Chr	Meth/COCU
Acts 1:15–26	Acts 1:15–17, 20–26	Acts 1:15–26 or Exod. 28:1–4, 9–10, 29–30	Acts 1:15–17, 21–26	Acts 1:15–26 or Exod. 28:1–4, 9–10, 29–30
1 John 4:13–21	1 John 4:11–16	1 John 5:9–15 or Acts 1:15–26	1 John 4:11–16	1 John 4:11–21
John 17:11b–19	John 17:11b–19	John 17:11b–19	John 17:11–19	John 17:11–19

EXEGESIS

First Lesson: Acts 1:15–26. In this story Luke portrays the earliest church in an interim period between the ascension and Pentecost, not yet guided by the Holy Spirit and no longer guided by the presence of Jesus. Hence the community, already clearly led by Peter, seeks God's own guidance in prayer and, in biblical fashion, interprets the casting of lots as a manifestation of the divine will. The whole passage is, in fact, written in noticeably "biblical" language—for Luke the language of the Septuagint Greek translation. Whatever historical tradition Luke had to work with, the passage as it stands is carefully composed and from it one can learn a great deal about Lucan methods of composition. For example, in the speech of Peter it is at least as much Luke addressing his readers as Peter his companions. Peter would have spoken Aramaic; he would hardly have needed to give his companions the explanation found in v. 19; and he would not have used scriptural arguments based only on the Septuagint version.

The speech contains a succession of interesting points, first regarding the function of scripture, which in early Christianity was reinterpreted to shed light not only on the meaning of Jesus but on any events surrounding him and the church itself. Thus scripture, through which the Holy Spirit speaks, had foretold both the fate of Judas (Ps. 69:25) and the action of the community (Ps. 109:8). As for the fate of Judas, Luke knows only a legend associated with the name of the Field of Blood. We find a very different legend with the same association in Matt. 27:3–10. Acts 1:21–22 provide what is virtually the definition of an apostle as one who accompanied the earthly Jesus from the beginning to the ascension (and thus Luke cannot allow Paul the title of apostle, Acts 14:4 and 14 notwithstanding). The concept of witness is a broader one, however, and could be extended to a larger group, as 13:31 implies, as well as to Paul.

In the Lucan writings prayer marks most important occasions, and this one is no exception. Instead of presuming to elect a successor to Judas, the community prays for God to choose between the two candidates who are put forward as presumably meeting the qualifications. As with most of the apostles, however, Matthias is not mentioned again in the narrative of Acts.

Second Lesson: 1 John 4:13–21. The concluding verses of 1 John 4 repeat, and in some cases carry further, the themes of the earlier part of the chapter, including its polemical context. They do so in often memorable and much-quoted language. V. 13 is very nearly a repetition of 3:24b. The following verse appeals to the testimony of the author in a manner reminiscent of the prologue to the Epistle; "seeing" is, of course, a kind of spiritual insight into the significance of Jesus. V. 15 is again a polemical statement recalling the test of faith by which the Johannine community is judged. The emphasis of the Christian confession in this formulation is most probably on Jesus. In light of 4:2–3 it is unlikely that the heretics deny the Son of God, but they deny that the Son of God is identical with the human Jesus.

V. 17, which again imposes the future eschatological criterion on the demand to love (cf. 2:28), presents the interpreter with a difficult problem. What is the meaning of the clause, "because as he is so are we in this world"? Suggestions have been varied, including the notion that the text is accidentally garbled, the phrase is misplaced, or it is a later gloss. But perhaps the idea is a simple one: the "he" in question refers to Christ who was and is the perfect exemplar of love; those who love as he did and does, though they are still in the world, resemble him in the maturity (or perfection) of their love. Love and fear of adverse eschatological judgment are incompatible, as v. 18 states. What is the love in question? It is, of course, love of God, inspired by the divine initiative of love for humanity (vv. 19–20). But love of God can be an airy abstraction as the heretics, who overspiritualize the love command, imply. With his feet solidly on the ground, the author of the Epistle relates love of God directly to love of one's fellow believer. This is the decisive mark of the loyal member of the community, one who has correctly understood Jesus' own command to love God and neighbor.

Gospel: John 17:11b–19. This passage is part of the eloquent prayer that concludes the Farewell Discourses of the Fourth Gospel, from the central section (vv. 6–19) in which Jesus prays for his disciples. Like other passages in the Farewell Discourses, it is written from a postresurrection perspective, which explains some of the past tenses and the viewpoint of Jesus' return to the Father in death. The repetition that marks the passage (e.g., vv. 11 and 12, 14 and 16) is characteristic of the discourse style of the Gospel.

Jesus prays that the Father will keep the disciples in his name as Jesus himself has done. It is not entirely clear what the phrase "in thy name" means precisely, and indeed it may be rather general in reference. The context suggests that it is a prayer to keep the disciples faithful to the revelation of God which Jesus was sent to make (cf. 14a: "I have given them thy word"). The last part of v. 11, "that they may be one, even as we are one," is not entirely textually sound and seems out of place since Jesus' formal prayer for unity will begin with v. 20. Reading the text as it stands, however, we may conclude that fidelity to the revelation of God in Christ is the source of unity among believers, a unity as intimate as that between the Son and the Father (cf. vv. 20–23).

The reference to the loss of Judas in v. 12 contains a play on the words "lost" and "perdition" in Greek. Though the "son of perdition" can refer to an eschatological figure of evil (as in 2 Thess. 2:3), here it probably means the one who was destined to be lost. It is the reinterpretation of Scripture (perhaps Ps. 41:9; cf. John 13:18) that reveals Judas's destiny—with no implications for the degree of his own responsibility.

Vv. 13–18 show us something more of the complex meaning of the term "world" in Johannine usage. It can mean both the place and the people who inhabit it. The world can be the object of God's love (3:16) or the adversary which Jesus has overcome (16:33). In our passage the word is generally used in a negative sense, as it is used frequently in the Farewell Discourses. But the disciples may not simply withdraw from the world. As Jesus was sent by the Father to bring revelation to the world and to challenge it to believe and thus to be saved, to have eternal life (cf. 3:16–17), so Jesus sends the disciples to carry on his mission of the revealing word (17:18). For this they must be set apart, made holy ("sanctify," v. 17; "consecrate," v. 19; note the unusual address with which the passage opens, "Holy Father," v. 11b, and see 10:36 for the consecration and sending of Jesus). Once made holy in truth, they will be set free and empowered by the truth to carry out their difficult mission. Jesus consecrates himself in death, the ultimate fulfillment of the Father's will for him. His death is thus implicitly sacrificial in character, but sacrifice is not the dominant element in Johannine soteriology. It is revelation that is emphasized.

HOMILETICAL INTERPRETATION

In older calendars, this Sunday was commonly called the Sunday after Ascension Day, and the traditional collect repeats the ascension

The Seventh Sunday of Easter

motif. Even the traditional lessons, however, did not pick up ascension themes but continued the pattern of late Easter season readings. Virtually the same thing is true in the case of the lessons with which we have to do under the present provisions. The First Lesson is a continuation of the narrative after the account of the ascension in Acts, but it has to do with the continuity of the church before the coming of the Spirit on Pentecost (see the exegesis). The Second Lesson, from 1 John, is part of the course of readings of this epistle which has been going on since the Fourth Sunday of Easter. The Gospel is another pericope from the Farewell Discourses.

The lessons, in other words, encourage the preacher to treat this Sunday as part of Easter. If the preacher feels it desirable to preach about the ascension and exaltation of Christ and his session at the right hand of God, it will be a doctrinal sermon drawn from resources other than these texts.

The readings themselves constitute at best a loose unity. Both the First Lesson and the Gospel have to do with God's care for the church after the death of Christ. The point of the reading from Acts seems to be the constitution of the identity of the church as the new Israel, through the filling up of the ranks of Apostles to the number of twelve after the death of Judas (Acts 1:26), presumably making the Twelve a "type" of the twelve sons of Jacob/Israel. The Eleven take this action by using the ancient Israelite device of casting lots, and the "biblical language" of the whole passage is obvious, as the exegesis points out. The thrust of the Gospel is toward the establishment of a unified and holy church, dedicated to the word of God in the world and consecrated for mission. The church is empowered for the duration of history. A sermon on the church as the people of God could be structured with two parts: a look to the past and to the roots of the Christian movement in Israel, and a look to the future and to the church's difficult problem of being in the world but not of it.

In this latter connection, the reading from 1 John becomes pertinent. The enigmatic phrase "as he is, so are we in this world" is illuminated by Jesus' prayer in the Gospel for the church not to be taken out of the world. For he was not taken out of the world. He was, in his lifetime, "a man of sorrows and acquainted with grief," yet his "love was perfected," he had "confidence for the day of judgment," and there was no fear in him. Perfect love casts out fear. So is the church to be in the conduct of its mission. "As he was, so are we in this world."

One also notices in both the First Lesson and the Gospel the emergence of the theme of prophecy and fulfillment. In the case of Acts it has to do with the death of Judas and his replacement in the apostolic band;

in the Gospel we read that the "son of perdition" was lost that "scripture might be fulfilled."

There is, of course, a mechanical and arbitrary way in which the OT can be combed to find precedents and foreshadowings of NT events. Sometimes the results of such a search are farfetched and implausible. On the other hand, if we believe that the life and death of Jesus of Nazareth is the definitive revelation of God in history and that Easter is the vindication of that divine communication, then the events of the gospel surely must illuminate all that has gone before, as the acts of God. In that case, of course, the proper interpretation of the sacred text of the Old Covenant will point to the finality of God's revelation in Christ. Prophecy and fulfillment in either sense is a most appropriate theme for the Easter season. If the preacher were to elect to deal with it on the Seventh Sunday of Easter, he or she might look at a number of the speeches in Acts, beginning with Acts 1:15–20 and including especially Stephen's speech before the Sanhedrin (where the element of reinterpretation of the OT is particularly obvious and results in Stephen's condemnation) to show how the new Christian community claims the old, old story of God's dealing with Israel as its own. The appointment of Matthias in the place of Judas is a crucial aspect of that claim. We have to do with a new version of the "twelve tribes."

First Lesson: Acts 1:15–26. We have already discussed the element of prophecy and fulfillment which constitutes such a prominent element of this passage.

More central to the meaning of the passage and to the meaning of the Easter season is provision for the leadership of the church by the power of the Spirit. The NT indicates three different ministries, each necessary for a different epoch of its life in the Spirit or for a different aspect of its work.

In the reconstitution of the Twelve by the appointment of Matthias, we recognize what might be called a "typological" ministry, making the church a type of Israel—the "Israel of God" (Gal. 6:16). The successor of Judas had to be "one of the men who accompanied us during all the time the Lord Jesus went in and out among us" (v. 21). He had to have known the Lord in the flesh, because by definition the Twelve could not be continued beyond the first generation. They could not be institutionalized.

There were apostles, however, who were not of the Twelve. Paul and Barnabas belonged to that number (Acts 14:4 et al.; see the exegesis). This "order of ministry," along with prophets, teachers, evangelists, and perhaps others (1 Cor. 12:28–29; Eph. 4:11) might be termed

The Seventh Sunday of Easter

"charismatic." We do not know how such persons were selected or ordained or whether the office was permanent. They seem to have constituted an itinerant ministry (Acts, Didache). This ministry met the needs of the church during the tumultuous early years, when the eschatological horizon was low and the end seemed imminent.

There were also bishops and elders (probably the same order at the beginning) and deacons. These orders provided the leadership for the local congregation, and have met the needs of the church during the prolonged period of history in which we find ourselves. We might call it the "institutional ministry." This ministry in turn has appeared in a number of forms in different denominations, but each denomination has claimed this third NT model as the basis for its institutional provisions.

On the basis of this analysis, we might see that there are *no* successors to the Apostles, if by that term the Twelve are designated. Christians who hold to "apostolic succession" may point to the historical continuity between apostles in the more general charismatic sense and bishops as inferred from the Didache; however, in doing so they should recognize the ambiguity of the term "bishop." Are not bishops and elders the same? Those who do not hold to "apostolic succession" should be sensitive to the need for an outward sign of faithfulness to the apostolic message and mission. The twentieth-century church is discovering that with respect to ministry, as in so many other ways, there are varieties of gifts by one Spirit.

Second Lesson: 1 John 4:13–21. This pericope continues to sound the themes familiar from earlier lections: abiding (3:6, 9, 24), the gift of the Spirit (3:24; 4:2), the confession of Jesus as Christ (4:2), confidence before God (3:21), the priority of God's love (4:9–10), and the new commandment that "he who loves God should love his brother also" (3:23; 4:7). The reader is asked to look at earlier sections of this volume for a discussion of those themes.

Two ideas are new here: "As he is so are we in this world" (v. 17) and "There is no fear in love, for perfect love casts out fear" (v. 18). We have already alluded to the first in our discussion of the posture of the church in the world. The second is the logical and powerful conclusion of the affirmation that Christians are to be confident in the Day of Judgment, because God abides in us and we in him as a result of the coming of the Son of God.

To say that love has cast out fear is one of the most general and universal ways of stating the whole gospel of Christ. It might be worth a sermon in itself. Strong as the emotion of fear is, love is stronger—or to be true to the text, the love of God is stronger, for it alone is unconditional and absolute. One does not fear death, judgment, guilt, or any of the more specific foes which confront us daily. As a point of departure, one might use one of several analogies: the way parental love imparts to parents the courage to defend their offspring; the bravery of weak nations in defending themselves from the predatory attacks of stronger ones, the power of a positive relationship in psychotherapy to heal anxieties and neurotic fears, or the ability to face down tremendous odds when empowered by strong desires or intense emotions. Revealing as such examples are, none is perfect love. Perfect love, revealed in the death of the Son of God for our sakes, casts out all fear.

Gospel: John 17:11b-19. This pericope is part of Jesus' high-priestly prayer, the climax of the Farewell Discourses. As the exegesis points out, it is written from a "postresurrection perspective" and hence is appropriate for this Easter season.

The high-priestly prayer is a prayer for the disciples. Unlike the First Lesson, which pertains to a moment in the life of the church that cannot be repeated, this reading seems directed to the church in every age. The verses in our lesson suggest five points:

First, the unity of the church. ". . . that they may be one, even as we (Father and Son) are one" (v. 11). The model of the unity of Christian disciples is the love which unites the persons of the Trinity. Such unity is not achieved by legislative schemes or enforced upon weaker groups by the greater power of one body of Christians. It is a unity in self-giving love, of which the only adequate symbol is the cross of Christ. Alternatively, it is a unity in the Holy Spirit. Necessary as canonical legislation is in a unified church and inevitable as the role of power is in the relation between any two bodies, neither factor can achieve the unity of the church. That unity is a relationship in love, effected in prayer in the Spirit.

Second, faithfulness to the word. "I have given them thy word. . . . Sanctify them in the truth; thy word is truth" (vv. 14, 17). This passage does not specify what "word" means. The rest of the Fourth Gospel would suggest that the word—or the Lord—is the revelation of the eternal God in Christ Jesus. Yet the phrase "I have given them thy word" suggests that something different from the incarnation is intended. The disciples have been entrusted with a meaning and a power which is the very truth of God, rooted in the life of the incarnate One, and yet permanently abiding with the disciples.

Third, tension between the church and the world (v. 14). Faithfulness to the word incurs the hostility of the world which is alienated from God (see above). Yet the role of the church is not to withdraw from the world

The Seventh Sunday of Easter

in a separatist and perfectionist way but to remain in the world, free from the evil one. God never lets the world go. He aims to reclaim it through his church.

Fourth, the church is holy, as Christ is holy. "And for their sake I consecrate myself, that they also may be consecrated in the truth" (v. 19). That is, the church is *not* holy in and of itself. The church is *made* holy by the atoning sacrifice of the Son. It is holy because it is God's, for the Son is God's and the church is the Son's (cf. 1 Cor. 3:23).

Fifth, the church is sent. "As thou didst send me into the world, so I have sent them into the world" (v. 18). The church has a mission, and in that sense is always apostolic, for "apostle" means one sent. Jesus was sent by God. The church is sent into the world by its Lord. Its ministry to the world, in faithfulness to the word, is the true continuation of the apostolic ministry.

In a brief, nontechnical, and unpolemical context we have here an early statement of the works of the church—that it is one, holy, catholic (here in the sense of being faithful to the universal truth of the Word), and apostolic.